Culture and Conflicts in Sierra Leone Mining

Culture and Conflicts in Sierra Leone Mining

Strangers, Aliens, Spirits

Fenda A. Akiwumi

ANTHEM PRESS

Anthem Press
An imprint of Wimbledon Publishing Company
www.anthempress.com

This edition first published in UK and USA 2024
by ANTHEM PRESS
75–76 Blackfriars Road, London SE1 8HA, UK
or PO Box 9779, London SW19 7ZG, UK
and
244 Madison Ave #116, New York, NY 10016, USA

© Fenda A. Akiwumi 2024

The author asserts the moral right to be identified as the author of this work.

All rights reserved. Without limiting the rights under copyright reserved above,
no part of this publication may be reproduced, stored or introduced into
a retrieval system, or transmitted, in any form or by any means
(electronic, mechanical, photocopying, recording or otherwise),
without the prior written permission of both the copyright
owner and the above publisher of this book.

British Library Cataloguing-in-Publication Data
A catalogue record for this book is available from the British Library.

Library of Congress Cataloging-in-Publication Data
A catalog record for this book has been requested.
2024930421

ISBN-13: 978-1-83998-809-7 (Hbk)
ISBN-10: 1-83998-809-6 (Hbk)

Cover Credit: William Vest-Lillesøe

This title is also available as an e-book.

In loving memory of:

My husband Akitoye A. Akiwumi (1935–2022), steadfast and devoted.

My parents Amelia Kendrick-Blyden (1928–2020) and
Edward W. Blyden III (1918–2010) who taught us well.

Uncle Tamba, Paramount Chief Tamba Songu Mbriwa (1910–1968),
sociocultural justice warrior.

My powerhouse female ancestors on whose shoulders
I stand: Great-Great Grandaunt Martha Ann Erskine-Ricks,
Great Grandma Anna Erskine, Great Grandaunt Lizzie Baker-Peel,
Nana Henrietta Maund—Kendrick, Grandaunt Jeanette Maund,
Grandma Isa Blyden, and Aunty Amina Jarrett.

CONTENTS

List of Figures and Tables	ix
Acknowledgements	xi
Abbreviations	xiii

1	Introduction: Culture in Commodity Chains	1
	Conceptual Model of a Culture-Centered Mineral Commodity Chain	13
	Methodology	16
2	Sierra Leone's Global Incorporation Through Mining	19
	Indigenous Artisanal Mining	20
	Mining in the Colonial and Postcolonial Eras	25
3	Cultural Difference: Policy and Legislative Dilemmas	35
	Ordinances and More Ordinances	41
	Cultural Resistance and Illicit Mining as Protest	52
4	Sacred Places: Local Ontology Meets Global Capital	63
5	Strangers, Environment, and Livelihoods	77
	Environmental Deterioration from Mining	79
	Women Own the Water—Cultural Disruption and Scoop-Net Fishing	88
	Mining Regulations and Cultural Sensitivity	91
6	Race, Ethnicity, Class, and Gender in Mining	97
	We Are the People Here: Land Rights, Hiring Practices, and CSR	102
	Women, Children, and Mining	107
7	Between a Rock and a Hard Place	111
8	Conclusion	115

References	119
Index	139

LIST OF FIGURES AND TABLES

Figures

1.1	Sierra Leone Provinces	2
1.2	Sierra Leone Districts	2
1.3	Sierra Leone Chiefdoms	3
1.4	A culture-centered mineral commodity chain model	13
2.1	Some major mineral occurrences	20
2.2	Sierra Leone waterways and lakes	21
2.3	Historic iron smelting furnace circa 1912–1914	26
3.1	Petition by Kono chiefs to Great Britain Colonial Office, 1957	46
4.1	Fetish fish pond, Kenema Town circa 1910	64
4.2	Sacred bush at Tefeya Village, Kono District, 2006	67
4.3	Sacred place in rutile lease, 1980s	69
5.1	Landscape of ponds, sand tailings, and slimes from rutile mining, 2005	83
5.2	Land use changes from rutile dredging, 1964–1990	83
5.3	Solondo dredge under construction, 2005	84
5.4	Dredge and wet plant on Lanti deposit	84
5.5	Rutile ore ready for shipment	85
5.6	Cassava cultivation on mine tailings, Moyamba District	86
5.7	Brick making using sand tailings and slimes	86
5.8	Women scoop-net fishing in mined-out Mogbwemo dredge pond	89
6.1	Wage labor at plant site, SRL Mine, 2005	98

Tables

2.1	Current special agreements for large-scale mining	32
3.1	Changes to traditional sociopolitical structures caused by mining	37
3.2	License holders in the gold mining industry and African labor, 1929–1944	39
3.3	Number of alluvial diamond dealers' licenses held by citizens and noncitizens, 1959–1971	40

ACKNOWLEDGEMENTS

This story has been a long time in the making and the process has taken a somewhat unconventional pathway/trajectory. I worked as a hydrogeologist at the Land and Water Development Division of the Ministry of Agriculture and Forestry in Sierra Leone (formerly the Land Resources Survey Project of the Food and Agricultural Organisation (FAO) of the United Nations) between 1978 and 1991. The work which was interdisciplinary and collaborative involved engagement with rural communities on water supply and agricultural projects. I learned the importance of a holistic approach to understanding and thinking about development issues. So I would like to acknowledge my colleagues at LWDD for their inspiration. The late Ahmed Songa Lamin, Mohamed "Pablo" Jalloh, Joe Hamelberg, Abubakar Jalloh, Osmond Gordon, Adama Conteh (RIP); Ambrose Williams, Frank Bassir, Christopher Jayakaran, Mohamed "Medo" Conteh, Isatu Khalu Wurie, Winston Allen, Daphne Awuta-Coker, Ansumana Kaikai, Hawa Wurie, Marie Umarr Kamarah, Dentuma Maligi, Isatu Sowe, and Yvonne John. But the heart of this book came out of my experiences working as part of the Environmental Scientific and Consulting Group (ESCG) with Ahmed Songa Lamin and Mohamed Conteh for Sierra Rutile Ltd. I am grateful to Andrew Karmoh Keili, then the company Mines Planning Engineer for advocating for Sierra Leonean professionals with firsthand knowledge of the local environment and culture to serve as consultants to the company. What started as a conversation on Sierra Leone mining development with Andrew on a day in 1986 at the Clubhouse at Mobimbi, SRL turned into almost 40 years of discussions and brainstorming. I greatly appreciate your tremendous support, encouragement, and input over many years. Thanks also to Tanimola Pratt, the late Alex Kamara, Haji Dabo, Ezekiel Kposowa, and D. J. Young, the General Manager from 1978 to 1988. Thank you, Don Young for your sensitivity to cultural heritage and the gift of slides and photographs depicting rural life and culture in the rutile mine lease, and your narrative on the Tegibeh Rice Growing Project. I acknowledge the women of *Muglomie* Cooperative at Kpetema Village for their fortitude, resilience, and resourcefulness.

xii CULTURE AND CONFLICTS IN SIERRA LEONE MINING

My experiences and observations in the mining areas culminated in a doctoral degree in Environmental Geography from Texas State University—San Marcos, USA, in 2006. I was fortunate to have two renowned geography scholars as co-advisors—David R. Butler and late Fred Shelley—and the illustrious David Stea on my dissertation committee. They strengthened my interdisciplinary perspective. I am particularly grateful to the late Lawrence E. Estaville, Geography Department Chair—professor, mentor, colleague, and friend for his classes in research design and geographic thought, and many intellectual discussions on development theories, culture, and environmental and social justice.

And to so many mentors and friends who supported me in one way or another with this project. Some gone but not forgotten are Karmoh Arthur Abraham, Florence Margai, Robert Treadwell, and Chinny Eccles-James (RIP); Thank you Ambe Njoh for your brilliance, wisdom, and guidance throughout the tenure and promotion processes at University of South Florida. Thanks also to Muriel Harris, Toyin Falola, Alusine Jalloh, Darlene Oceana Gutierrez, Dawna Cerney, David Viertel, Sigismond Wilson, Onipede Arthur Hollist, Kashope Handel Wright, Cyril Wilson, Lorenzo D'Angelo, Earl Conteh-Morgan, Isata Hyde, Ibipo Johnston—Anumunwo, Roxanne Watson, Nalinie Kouame, and Michael Acheampong.

Thank you, Andrew Keili, Charles "Chip" Stanish, and Nemata Blyden for reading the draft and giving feedback; Faye Ricker for proofreading the manuscript; the three reviewers for their very encouraging feedback; Maxine Haspel for drawing the provinces, districts, and drainage maps and Akiyele Akiwumi for the mineral map; William Vest Lillesoe, Estelle Levin-Nally, Donald J. Young, and Peter Andersen for the use of photographs. Last but not least, my dear children Akiyele, Akilade, and Olubumi, my joy and motivation; and my dearly loved siblings and their families. Babatunde (RIP), Isa, Bai Bureh, Henrietta (Coker), Eluem (Cozin), Eddie (Didi),-Nemata, and I were nurtured in a thought-provoking environment full of love, empathy, and compassion.

ABBREVIATIONS

ADMS	Alluvial Diamond Mining Scheme
AGMS	Alluvial Gold Mining Scheme
AML	African Minerals Ltd.
ASM	Artisanal and Small-Scale Mining
AU	African Union
CDA	Community Development Agreement
CDW	Colonial Development and Welfare
CSR	Corporate Social Responsibility
EIA	Environmental Impact Assessment
EITI	Extractive Industries Transparency Initiative
EPA-SL	Environment Protection Agency-Sierra Leone
ESHIA	Environmental, Social and Health Impact Assessment
FDI	Foreign Direct Investment
MNC	Multinational Corporation
NLP	National Land Policy
RUF/SL	Revolutionary United Front of Sierra Leone
SEPL	Special Exclusive Prospecting Lease
SLDC	Sierra Leone Development Company
SLEITI	Sierra Leone Extractive Industries Transparency Initiative
SLGS	Sierra Leone Geological Survey
SLST	Sierra Leone Selection Trust
SRL	Sierra Rutile Ltd.

Chapter 1

INTRODUCTION:
CULTURE IN COMMODITY CHAINS

In the whole history of economic activity the stranger makes his appearance everywhere as a trader, and the trader makes his as a stranger.[...] The stranger is by his very nature no owner of land.[...] Although in the sphere of intimate personal relations the stranger may be attractive and meaningful in many ways, so long as he is regarded as a stranger he is no "landowner" in the eyes of the others. (Georg Simmel in Levine 1971, 144)

In this book, 1 demonstrate that the low-level mining area conflicts of sub-Saharan African countries, such as Sierra Leone, and their influences on mineral policy, law, and development fundamentally stem from cultural conundrums. Cultural differences in the conceptualization of land rights, and land use and management between the state and the customary authority are inherent in mineral commodity chains causing conflicts. I emphasize that the customary landlord–stranger institution and its cultural underpinnings are central to an understanding of mining conflicts in Sierra Leone. I examine how the state addresses cultural differences in mining, and land governance, more generally. The book is a contribution to the world system research on culture in commodity chains, the literature on African mining conflicts, and the anthropology and social and environmental mining history of Sierra Leone.

Sierra Leone is located on the west coast of Africa with a land area of about 72,000 square kilometers, about the size of Ireland. The country is bordered by Guinea to the north and Liberia to the south. Politically it is divided into 5 provinces, 16 districts, and 190 chiefdoms (Figures 1.1–1.3). Under British colonial rule that ended in 1961, the area comprised The Colony (now Western Area) and the Protectorate. Sierra Leone became a Republic in 1971. The population is approximately 8.5 million made up of several ethnic groups (Temne, Mende, Limba, Kono, Korankoh, Fullah, Mandingo, Loko, Sherbro, Susu, Kissi, Krim, Vai, and Yalunka) and Krio (Creole) descendants

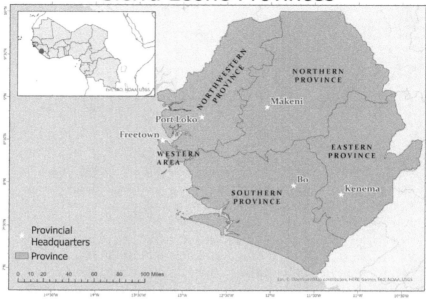

Figure 1.1 Sierra Leone Provinces.

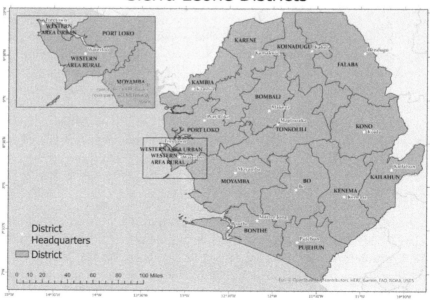

Figure 1.2 Sierra Leone Districts.

INTRODUCTION

Sierra Leone Chiefdoms

KAILAHUN
Dea
Jahn
Jawie
Kissi Kama
Kissi Teng
Kissi Tongi
Kpeje Bongre
Kpeje West
Luawa
Malema
Mandu
Njaluahun
Penguia
Upper Bambara
Yawei

FALABA
Delemandugu
Dembelia
Dembelia-Sinkunia
Folosaba
Kamadu Yiraia
Kebelia
Kulor Saradu
Mongo
Morifindugu
Neya
Nyedu
Sulima
Wollay Barawa

KARENE
Buya
Dibia
Gbanti
Libeisaygahun
Mafonda Makerembay
Romende
Safroko
Sanda Loko
Sanda Magbolontor
Sanda Tendaran
Sella Limba
Tambakha Simibungie
Tambakha Yobangie

MOYAMBA
Bagruwa
Bumpeh
Dasse
Fakunya
Kagboro
Kaiyamba
Kamajei
Kongbora
Kori
Kowa
Lower Banta
Ribbi
Timdale
Upper Banta

KENEMA
Dama
Dodo
Gaura
Gorama Mende
Kandu Leppiama
Koya
Langrama
Lower Bambara
Malegohun
Niawa
Nomo
Nongowa
Simbaru
Small Bo
Tunkia
Wandor
Kenema City

KOINADUGU
Diang
Gbonkobon Kayaka
Kalian
Kamukeh
Kasunko KaKellian
Nieni
Sengbe
Tamiso
Wara Wara Bafodia
Wara Wara Yagala

PORT LOKO
Bakeh Loko
Bureh
Kaffu Bullom
Kamasondo
Kasseh
Koya
Lokomasama
Maconteh
Maforki
Makama
Marampa
Masimera
Thainkatopa

PUJEHUN
Barri
Galliness
Kabonde
Kpaka
Makpele
Malen
Mono Sakrim
Panga
Panga krim
Pejeh
Perri
Soro Gbema
Sowa
Yakemu Kpukumu

KONO
Fiama
Gbane
Gbane Kandor
Gbense
Gorama Kono
Kamara
Lei
Mafindor
Nimikoro
Nimiyama
Sandor
Soa
Tankoro
Toli
Koidu City

TONKOLILI
Dansogoia
Gbonkolenkeni
Kafe
Kalanthuba
Kholifa Mabang
Kholifa Mamuntha
Kholifa Rowala
Kunike Barina
Kunike Folawusu
Kunike Sanda
Malal
Mayeppoh
Poli
Sambaya
Simiria
Tane
Yele
Yoni Mabanta
Yoni Mamaila

BO
Badjia
Bagbo
Bagbwe(Bagbe)
Boama
Bongor
Bumpe Ngao
Gbo
Jaiama
Kakua
Komboya
Lugbu
Niawa Lenga
Selenga
Tikonko
Valunia
Wonde
Bo Town

WESTERN RURAL
Koya Rural
Mountain Rural
Waterloo Rural
York Rural

BOMBALI
Biriwa
Bombali Sebora
Bombali Siari
Gbanti
Gbendembu
Kamaranka
Magbaimba
Makari
Mara
N'gowahun
Paki Masabong
Safroko Limba
Makeni City

KAMBIA
Bramaia
Dixon
Gbinle
Khonimaka
Magbema
Mambolo
Masungbala
Muna Thalla
Samu
Tonko Limba

BONTHE
Bendu-Cha
Bum
Dema
Imperri
Jong
Kpanda Kemo
Kwamebai Krim
Nongoba Bullom
Sittia
Sogbeni
Yawbeko
Bonthe Urban

WESTERN URBAN
Central I
Central II
East I
East II
East III
West I
West II
West III

Figure 1.3 Sierra Leone Chiefdoms.

of freed slaves resettled in Freetown in the late eighteenth to early nineteenth centuries. Women make up 51 percent of the population. Around 44 percent of the population lives in urban areas.

During the colonial era, Sierra Leone comprised The Colony, the present-day Western Area, and the Protectorate (current Provincial Area). The Colony was governed by English Common Law and the Protectorate by Native Law and Custom and various colonial modifications of that decentralized traditional governance system. Adaptations to the traditional governance system occurred through the Protectorate Land Ordinance of 1905, which created the Tribal or Native Authority (now Chiefdom Councils). These traditional governing bodies comprise Paramount chiefs, political heads of chiefdoms, chiefs, councilors, and selected village elders. The colonial legacy of a dual governance system remains. The state continues to govern through statutes that supersede native law and custom (Ochiai 2017).

The Sierra Leonean government, like many developing sub-Saharan nations, today, depends heavily on mineral extraction for foreign exchange revenue. Sierra Leone is rich in a variety of minerals including several strategic and critical materials essential for national defense and modern technologies (IEA 2023; United States Govt. 2023). Guided by international entities such as the World Bank, Sierra Leone has historically devised policies and laws to encourage foreign direct investment (FDI) in the mining sector, protect mineral commodity chains, and ensure mineral supply to global markets. Mining revenue finances the government's development plans, the Agenda for Prosperity, 2013–2018 and the Medium Term National Development Plan, 2019–2023 (New Direction). Although the Ebola crisis in early 2014 impacted plans when some large-scale, capital-intensive mines shut down, Sierra Leone continues to encourage FDI with investor-friendly economic and legislative incentives. Artisanal, small-scale, and large-scale industrial mining operate concurrently in the country (EITI 2021; Govt. of Sierra Leone 2015a, 2015b, 2019; Mining Journal 2018).

Commodity chains facilitate the extraction of mineral resources and their exportation to global markets for the processing and production of goods in sub-Saharan African countries such as Sierra Leone. Such commodity chains, more generally, are vehicles through which peripheral countries, many of them in Africa, become incorporated into the global economy, often in a process of economic unequal exchange. Economic unequal exchange is the amount of labor time under low wage conditions invested by workers in a peripheral developing country to produce commodities traded between that country and developed core countries, for example, those in Western Europe. Peripheral countries, then, are exporting more embodied labor than they are importing as global commodity chains incorporate socioeconomic

INTRODUCTION

impacts such as cheap labor exploitation in traded goods (Boatcă et al. 2017; Korzeniewicz 2018; Simas et al. 2015; Wallerstein 1983). Embodied labor means the actual labor expended by workers and their labor time is embodied in the commodities they extract or produce.

Concerning Africa, Walter Rodney (1981) explained how the colonial state transformed class and labor structures to gain political and economic power. Europeans controlled industrial enterprise and offered very low wages to African laborers. State legislation supported such policy and the use of force to manage discontent by labor over working conditions. In the mines and the civil service, white employees were paid on a higher salary scale than their African counterparts.

Multinational Corporations (MNCs) with headquarters based in wealthy core regions such as the United States and Western Europe and increasingly semi-peripheral China are key players in commodity chain dynamics. The MNCs are vectors of capital in peripheral countries where their operations occur and exploit local labor in these distant places as part of global commodity chains. The hierarchical organizational structure of the modern MNC worldwide is a coercive form of institutionalized power equal to or exceeding that of hegemonic states themselves, oftentimes, negatively impacting peripheral countries where they operate (Bair 2009; Dunaway 2010; Li 2021; Thrift and Taylor 2013; Wallerstein 2000).

In addition to such manifestations of economic unequal exchange, natural resource extraction through commodity chains causes environmental degradation. World system researchers conceptualize this degradation as ecological unequal exchange (or unequal ecological exchange) where commodity chains embody land resources such as minerals from the periphery flowing to the core and resulting in environmental degradation in the periphery (Bunker 2019; Frey et al. 2019; Jorgenson and Clark 2012; Rice 2007). Liam Downey et al. (2010, 418) further theorized the interrelationship between armed violence and control over natural resources in the periphery by core nations and corporations as a primary cause of ecological unequal exchange. Moreover, the authors highlight the sociocultural and political dimensions of these natural resource conflicts as "complex social arrangements that are instituted, organized, shaped, directed, and controlled by specific organizations, institutions, treaties, and laws" to facilitate this exchange.

The Sierra Leone state's industrial development initiatives, which depend on foreign multinational company investments, therefore, conflict with customary land use and governance. This colonial legacy impacts land rights and the subsistence land-based livelihoods of indigenous people. Loss of land to externally generated projects impacts farming but may also include forfeiture of rights to practice artisanal mining and smelting of ores,

6   CULTURE AND CONFLICTS IN SIERRA LEONE MINING

centuries-old customary livelihoods in Sierra Leone and other West African countries. Many modern iron, gold, and copper mines in Africa are located at sites previously mined in precolonial times by indigenous Africans (Govt. of Sierra Leone 1935; Panella 2010; Perinbam 1988; Werthmann 2006). Such inequities stifle economic opportunities for local people and ensuing conflicts limit overall development.

Incorporation, the absorption of peoples and regions into the world system, embraces the tenets of what Immanuel Wallerstein (1983) called the "capitalist civilizational project." Wilma Dunaway (2003) summarized these tenets as including "universalization of culture and knowledge production" (3). Indigenous people, most often residing in rural areas, are caught up in commodity chains as labor, a situation that distorts households including their gender dynamics and socioeconomic and cultural sustainability. Some world system scholars compellingly contend that cultural disruption, particularly alienation from long established ways of life and ensuing cultural hybridity, is the most dire consequence of incorporation (e.g. Chase-Dunn 2018; Dunaway 2014, 2003; Smith and Ward 2000).

While interactive compromises, including the cooptation of a local agency, result from opposition to foreign hegemony, attempts to dominate indigenous peoples are still met with resistance as they struggle to maintain their civilizations and cultural heritages (Dunaway 2010; Hall and Fenelon 2015). Local households, then, are also "arenas that transmit culture and ethnic heritage and they are units that support and/or organize antisystemic resistance" (Dunaway 2001, 7–8). Cultural struggles, however, will be endless because of the continuing geographical expansion to exploit natural resources in peripheral places to satisfy global overconsumption (Dunaway 2003). I argue in support of Dunaway's (2003) view that while the incorporation of indigenous people caught up in commodity chains as labor pressures them into cultural and national assimilation, incorporation "is never complete and is always subject to resistance" (7, 12). The incorporation process, therefore, rather than unequivocally achieving cultural universalism in peripheral places bolsters indigenism and ethnification in response to the discontent that potentially threatens the capitalist civilizational project. Dunaway (2003) optimistically opined that continuing antisystemic and cultural resistance can potentially force systemic change in the world system. The resistance to a universal capitalist culture persists even though the developing peripheral state driven by a universal agenda and global markets facilitates incorporation through centralized control of resources (Hechter 2000).

My goal, in addition to highlighting cultural dynamics, is to develop a conceptual argument that cultural unequal exchange occurs in commodity chain processes. An asymmetric transfer of cultural resources and norms from

INTRODUCTION

core to periphery leads to the denigration, marginalization, or loss of local cultural heritage and involuntary or forced cultural evolution in the periphery. For example, the states' support of FDI in land development threatens African customary land governance systems such as the centuries-old landlord–stranger (tutor at-tuteur or stranger-father) institution. This historic mode of land governance determines how outsiders, or strangers, with no ancestral rights to land in a given place, can access land and land resources, or trade opportunities as determined by landlords (sometimes called *maitres de la terre*), indigenes of a place. Sacred places play a vital role in community cohesion, cultural continuity, livelihoods, and land-use rights. Landlord-indigene communities spring from village founders who might be famous hunters, warriors, or migrant farmers. Establishing ancestral burial grounds and other revered places tied them to the land as well as their descendants, and future generations (Dorjahn and Fyfe 1962; Falola 1985; Konneh 1996; Lentz 2013; Mouser 1980; Njoh 2006).

The institution collaborates with traditional power associations to determine how, and by whom, land resources and trade opportunities are accessed. Power associations in Sierra Leone include *Poro, Wunde,* and *Gbangbani* for men and *Sande* or *Bondo/u* for women. Members of societies include the Paramount chief as political and spiritual head, sub-chiefs, and individuals who possess craftsmanship such as herbalists and blacksmiths. Since craft specialists depend on land-based ecological and mineral resources, they have a say in land management decisions and are considered to have access to the forces of nature and spirit ancestors. These organizations are also referred to as secret societies or sodalities and are hierarchical religio-political and administrative organizations. They instill discipline and maintain law and order primarily by the use of sanctions, sometimes called medicine laws, or fetish regulations (Abraham 2003; Freudenberger et al. 1997).

Historically, landlords with ancestral rights to land host and protect a variety of strangers including traders, in-migrant farmers, pastoralists, hunters, artisans, artisanal miners, envoys or rulers, marabouts, musicians, uprooted migrants, herbalists, and healers. Traders were particularly welcome when West African Mande traders moved southward for commerce as far back as the eleventh century. Later, seafaring Portuguese explorers in the sixteenth century and their Luso-African descendants became a new type of stranger. In return, landlords received first rights to trade with strangers and/or entitlement to a portion of the stranger's profits. Also, strangers accessing land must pay tribute, the annual customary gift to both the ruling chief of the community as custodians of the land and their landlords. There is, therefore, a connection between kinship rights to land and benefits from facilitating trade. Strangers might reside on a long-term basis or marry into

8 CULTURE AND CONFLICTS IN SIERRA LEONE MINING

families in host communities. In post-conflict societies such as Sierra Leone following the Revolutionary United Front of Sierra Leone (RUF/SL) war period, strangers in various parts of the country may also include refugees, ex-combatants, and internally displaced people (Brooks 2003; Brooks and Beauregard 1993; Unruh 2008).

During the colonial period, the African state commodified land and made it available to external land investors for extractive industries. This policy impacted the intricate interrelationships between subsistence land-based livelihoods ontologically linked to ancestral sacred places and the cultural sustainability of landlord-indigene communities (Cormier-Salem and Bassett 2007; von Benda-Beckmann 1997; Werthmann 2006). Cultural changes continue to threaten traditional perceptions of the land. As Pauline Peters (2004, 305) explained "as land becomes a property or a commodity, so we see developing a very different sense of 'belonging'—from someone belonging to a place to a property belonging to someone; in short, a shift from inclusion to exclusion." Treating land as a commodity not only modified the landlord–stranger relationship, but exacerbated power and class differences; ethnic conflicts regarding autochthony and citizenship (Dorman et al. 2007) race relations (Sylvain 2015), gender (Verma 2014), generational, and kinship (Amanor 2010) dynamics.

European colonialists had a poor understanding of the world views underpinning traditional governance and dismissed practices as primitive, superstitious, or witchcraft. Moore and Sanders (2001, 3) write that such occult practices and discourses are not unique to Africa or indicative of primitive behavior; rather, "they can be explained with socioeconomic transformation, growing inequalities and the perceptions of modernity and globalization by local actor[s]." Marginalized peoples respond in different ways to asymmetrical power relations and economic, environmental, and sociocultural changes brought by externally introduced extractive activities. In an African context, change, according to Frank (1995), causes the adaptation of traditional ontological ideas about witchcraft to explain and understand the new political, socioeconomic, and cultural circumstances and environmental relationships. Mining is an important manifestation of global processes that affect local communities in distant places. Wealth accumulation and inequitable distribution of resources from minerals may cause jealousy and accusations of witchcraft from others. Cultural interpretations of change caused by mining impact gender relationships. Women are sometimes seen as the source of ill luck for men seeking wealth from minerals with poor outcomes. Witchcraft accusations become a means of curtailing any success women might achieve from other economic opportunities presented by mining (D'Angelo 2014, 2019; Rosen 1981).

INTRODUCTION

Colonization denigrated indigenous knowledge systems and realities of colonized peoples while imposing the colonizer's ideology. The ensuing Eurocentric (or Western-centric) knowledge production and representation prevails in the postcolonial period (Baker et al. 1996; Hall 1996; Williams and Chrisman 1994). The continuing power politics around such knowledge production and representation challenge the reemergence of other viewpoints (Baker et al. 1996). Other researchers see the potential for reconceptualizing development that integrates indigenous knowledge (Briggs and Sharp 2004; Mapara 2009). However, Mannathukkaren (2010, 307) cautioned about "the predatory universalism of western modernity" and reminded us that in a capitalist world culture and materialism are intricately linked. Capitalism imposes constraints on cultural expression. As such powerless groups in the economic hierarchy are caught up in a universal capital-driven modernity that might co-exist with precapitalist vestiges of exploitation and oppression.

In reflecting on such cultural conundrums in an African context, postcolonial thinkers underline the difficulty of defining a pure and universal African culture or customary norm concerning land or other sectors. The persistent dominance of a capitalist Western-centric worldview, a legacy of colonialism, continuously threatens African cultural expression and a common heritage to protect and harness for the continent's overall development planning. Colonial authorities ignored the diversity of customs from the precolonial era, choosing to select amenable chiefs as bearers of custom and empowering them through ordinances to take an authoritarian approach to govern. Such colonial ordinances modified and weakened the underpinnings of the landlord–stranger institution. Despite the imposition of colonial values on traditional leadership and customs, the institution persists and governs rural African communities at the local level (Ahluwalia 2012; Chanock 2006; Mamdani 2000; Obeng-Odoom 2015a, 2015b).

The African Union (AU) at the regional level recognizes the importance of the landlord–stranger institution's tenets for traditional rural societies. The AU's Framework and Guidelines on Land Policy in Africa emphasized that for land policy in Africa to succeed, it must address the intricate connection between land and spirituality:

> Land remains an important factor in the construction of social identity, the organization of religious life, and the production and reproduction of culture. The link across generations is ultimately defined by the complement of land resources which families, lineages, and communities share and control. Indeed land is fully embodied in the very spirituality of society. (African Union 2010, 8)

10 CULTURE AND CONFLICTS IN SIERRA LEONE MINING

The landlord–stranger institution's customary laws operate alongside but subordinate to statutory ordinances and laws introduced during the colonial era (African Union 2010; Govt. of Sierra Leone 2015c). Consequently, inherent cultural conflict exists between the landlord–stranger institution operating at the local level and the state (national) and global collaborative land use and natural resource extractive agendas. In some West African nations, artisanal mining as a customary livelihood complementing subsistence farming is, to some extent, still governed by customary laws through the landlord–stranger institution. However, the marginalization of this livelihood and loss of land rights are the cause of intractable conflicts between landlord communities and foreign mining MNCs operating in countries like Sierra Leone.

Shack and Skinner (1979, 13) contended that during the colonial era, the MNC became the hegemonic "new" stranger "exercising powerful control over the key economic sectors of African states and often engaging overtly in manipulating the political machinery of government." The MNC as a hegemonic stranger establishment appropriates land, usurps customary landlord rights and roles, and through its activities creates a hierarchy of strangers within, for example, Sierra Leone mining areas.

Georg Simmel's 1908 conceptualization of the stranger, since extended by subsequent scholars, is useful in my analysis of categories and hierarchies of strangers in Sierra Leone mining areas and conflicts. Strangers include a settler in a new environment, the newcomer, the sojourner who adheres to the culture of his ethnicity, and the one who disrespects the cultural norms of the host society (Gudykunst 1983; Levine 1977; Rogers 1999; Stonequist 1937). The marginal man is one "vulnerable to internal uncertainties" (Boskoff 1969, 282) or one who finds ways to adapt to community life in alien environments (Rose 1967). Other strangers fall into the category of "the rootless alien an ideal servant of power who can easily be bent to the ruler's purposes because he is totally dependent and cannot accumulate autonomous power" (Coser 1972, 574).

Consequently, stranger receptivity, genuine or coerced, links to the real or perceived political, economic, and sociocultural structural position of strangers. Landlord communities express a wide range of emotions toward strangers and stranger establishments that include ambivalence, antagonism, fear, hostility, indifference, and even friendliness, as situations dictate in space and time. This ambiguity about strangers can cast them as allies, pawns, or enemies, and strangers have often been uncomplicated targets of anger in response to inequities (Shack and Skinner 1979).

In the context of African societies and the stranger issue, Mamdani's (1996) views align with the world system premise of cultural resistance to external

INTRODUCTION

dominance. Despite the changes facilitated by the hegemonic state's economic agenda, including related legal reforms that drive capitalist modernity, "for every notion of the customary defined and enforced by the state, one could find a counter notion with a subaltern currency" (299). Traditional African communities, naturally, hold steadfast to the landlord–stranger institution's norms, especially where activities such as mining threaten communities' rights to lands and benefits accruing from land resources such as minerals.

The stranger is also embroiled in a history of violence over land rights and conflicts may ensue on a larger scale extending beyond individual landlords and strangers to entire landlord and stranger communities. Politicians have frequently used the stranger issue to their advantage for economic exclusion and political domination, turning economic strife over land into ethnic strife (Geschiere 2010; Utas 2012).

Specific to mining areas in African countries, strangers may have long histories of residency (Dummett 1998), be deliberately recruited for labor as in South Africa (Cronje and Chenga 2009), or be voluntary in-migrants seeking economic opportunities. The relationship between landlord-indigenes and strangers in mining communities varies from accommodation as in the tin mines of Nigeria (Freund 1981), through antagonism as in South Africa (Cronje and Chenga 2009), to outright hostility and targeted violence as in the Katanga Province of the Democratic Republic of the Congo (Nzongola-Ntalaja 2007). Occasionally, landlords control stranger mining activities through the use of customary land management strategies in collaboration with traditional leaders and earth priests in, for example, Mali (Grätz and Werthmann 2012).

Integrating the landlord–stranger paradigm and postcolonialism with a world system approach to commodity chain analysis of culture is thus useful for a fine-grained understanding of outcomes of commodity chains beyond economic unequal exchange and ecological unequal exchange. As Bair (2005) underscored, the world system conceptualization of commodity chains takes a historical, "macro and holistic perspective" (164). Using an African mineral commodity chain case study, my objectives in this book are in line with Bair's (2005) proposition that research on commodity chains should evolve to focus on "the factors external to chains that shape their geography and configuration and strongly affect the extent to which different actors benefit from participation in them" (167). I argue, however, that in my Sierra Leone case study, illicit extraction by local artisanal miners considered an external factor is, in fact, *internally* embedded within the officially designated commodity chain. This accounts for a distorted chain configuration with concomitant and varying outcomes for actors such as the state, MNCs, powerful and marginalized stranger groups, landlord-indigenes, local artisanal miners, and households. I support the premise that artisanal mining, oftentimes, categorized by the state as illicit and operating in the informal sector is, in some ways, a form of cultural resistance by landlord-indigene communities underscoring their customary claims to land resources (Conteh 1979; Hayward 1972). Sometimes, resistance manifests as violence, which can sometimes erupt into a full-scale war such as the RUF/SL Blood Diamond War from 1991 to 2001. I also concur with Bair's (2005) contention that addressing the factors that shape commodity chains will increase our understanding of their role in unequal development, a feature of global capitalism.

In interrogating the impacts of global capitalism, researchers of the Latin American periphery propose "neoextractivism" as an alternative development trajectory. In this paradigm, the state more effectively regulates the appropriation of natural resources and their export by MNCs. As such, the state benefits politically, socially, and economically and can ultimately achieve national sovereignty (Burchardt and Dietz 2014). Extraction policies and laws must be culturally sensitive and embody indigenous worldviews on human–nature interactions such as *Vivir bien or Buen vivir* (living well). The resulting development pathway should not endorse the commodification of social life and nature but embrace processes of territoriality, negotiation, cultural resistance, and mobilization when indigenous communities challenge a state's continuing capitalist development agenda. Negotiations between stakeholders need not necessarily exclude activities like mining but involve more equitable resource sharing with communities whose lands are impacted (Gudynas 2016; Savino 2016; Svampa 2019). Several studies on neoextractivism in Ecuador report mixed success rates and development outcomes (Falconer 2019; Goeury 2021; Williford 2018). For example, Villalba-Eguiluz and Etxano (2017) see neoextractivism and Buen vivir as incompatible.

Due to the importance of mineral resources in African development, some governments do support neoextractivism as a development trajectory guided by the African Union's Africa Mining Vision (AMV) 2030. Greco (2020) contends that African neoextractivism primarily encourages FDI investment through favorable agreements with multinational companies, revised mining legislation, and investment in structural transformation and social policies and programs. While lacking a cultural concept like *vivir bien*, Ziai (2017) proposed that the South African concept of *Ubuntu* embracing respect for human dignity and collective action may have similar potential in an African model. Edozie and Gottschalk (2014) conceptualized the AU Phenomenon drawing from Agenda 2063, a framework for development in Africa. Particularly, aspiration 5 of 7 is for "an Africa with a strong cultural identity, common heritage values, and ethics" (African Union 2016b). These virtues will serve as a foundation for alternative modernity in the face of growing external pressure for universal modernity (African Union 2016a).

I developed a combined conceptual framework integrating world system cultural perspectives of commodity chains, postcolonial notions of the subaltern and indigenous knowledge systems versus Eurocentrism, ethnic identity, and tenets of the landlord–stranger institution (e.g., Edozie and Gottschalk 2014; Mamdani 1996 and others) to interrogate the cultural dynamics (cultural resistance, cultural alienation, cultural disruption, cultural hybridity, and cultural evolution) inherent in world system commodity chains.

Conceptual Model of a Culture-Centered Mineral Commodity Chain

The conceptual framework for the book, a unidirectional mineral commodity chain model, highlights cultural dimensions (Figure 1.4). The model is built on world system perspectives of commodity chains, postcolonial notions of the subaltern, indigenous knowledge systems versus Eurocentrism (Western-centrism), ethnic identity, cultural evolution, and tenets of the African landlord–stranger relationship in land governance. The chain comprises four main links: (1) externally generated mining, (2) labor and extraction, (3) exportation, and (4) global markets. The model represents Sierra Leone mining from its inception in the early 1930s to the present and shows how both externally generated, capital-intensive operations by foreign mining MNCs and artisanal and small-scale mining (ASM) draw in the labor of

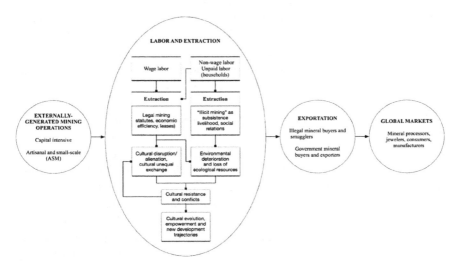

Figure 1.4 A culture-centered mineral commodity chain model.

14   CULTURE AND CONFLICTS IN SIERRA LEONE MINING

landlord host communities and their households and in-migrants (strangers). Such labor includes professional mine employees and low-paid mine wage labor, and the non-waged and unpaid labor of men, women, and children. Cultural dynamics permeate the labor-extraction link in the chain. These dynamics encompass both imposed Western cultural concepts of legal mining governed by statutes as economically efficient and indigenous mining as a poorly managed illicit practice. This view dominates, despite the latter practice being a historic subsistence livelihood embedded in social relations such as landlord–stranger reciprocities.

The imposition of Western concepts of mining and land use leads to cultural resistance, cultural disruption, and cultural alienation. Mining, whether legal or illicit, causes environmental degradation, desecration of sacred places, loss of ecological resources, and associated customary livelihoods, and threatens the sustainability of households. All these issues impact the efficacious operation of mineral commodity chains and result in chain distortion, thereby exacerbating cultural disruption and alienation that, in turn, cause continuous conflicts and resistance at extraction sites. Conflict and resistance by landlord-indigenes, however, periodically force the state to revise policies, such as devising avenues for their legal participation in artisanal mining or requiring greater corporate social responsibility by MNCs. The model explores the potential for forms of cultural evolution that might give rise to new livelihood opportunities in the mining sector and development trajectories.

Amid cultural conflicts, minerals such as gold and diamonds are extracted, smuggled, and exported both legally and illegally to global markets where they are processed and crafted for consumption. The national government loses significant revenue to illicit activity in the alluvial minerals sectors. Large-scale companies face protests and strikes, destruction of company property, and theft of materials that impact production timelines from time to time. While the majority of local miners and strangers generally make a meager living in mining areas, powerful middlemen, some traditional leaders, and government officials benefit more from extraction.

Illicit activity is frequently seen as operating at the margins of the government's officially prescribed commodity chain, thereby resulting in a complex configuration. Alternatively, illicit activity is seen as constituting a separate chain (Levin and Gberie 2006; Villegas et al. 2013). My model, however, highlights that illicit mining as a culturally driven factor is embedded within rather than external to the chain challenging smooth operations of the chain. Even in constant turmoil, meager gains for the majority of miners, and national government efforts to shut down illicit operations, artisanal mining survives as a historic and cultural livelihood. Difficulties government and MNCs face in unraveling the distorted commodity chain are

INTRODUCTION 15

not solely because of reactions by labor (legal and illegal) and households to an incorporation process that causes economic unequal exchange and ecological unequal exchange but also cultural unequal exchange. Policy and law do not effectively embody culturally diverse perspectives about livelihood opportunities and cultural expression in Sierra Leone's mining sector.

The Sierra Leone government has made efforts to reform land and mining policy and laws with colonial vestiges still embedded and align itself with international and African regional legal instruments. The Sierra Leone Minerals Policy 2018 and the Mines and Mineral Development Act 2021 draw from global and regional initiatives in mineral sector development. These include the AMV, the Kimberley Process Certification Scheme, the Natural Resource Charter, Economic Community of West African States (ECOWAS) Mining Directives, UN Guiding Principles for Business and Human Rights (UNGP), the African Charter on Human and Peoples' Rights, IFC Performance Standards on Environmental and Social Sustainability, and the Extractive Industries Transparency Initiative (EITI).

Interestingly, the AMV while appreciating the importance of artisanal mining as a crucial rural livelihood and income generator for African populations does not address the cultural dimensions of the sector. For example, the importance of customary governance in land disbursement and artisanal mining organization is minimized. However, a major goal is to formalize this reputed informal sector activity for local economic development (African Union 2010). I contend that the informal mining sector can be conceived as customary mining marginalized at the periphery of large-scale operations under mine leases.

Recent fieldwork on gold mining in Niger revealed that despite policies, laws, and programs to manage and formalize ASM, miners continue to "operate under unrecorded customary laws" (Hilson et al. 2017, 86). Perinbam (1988) reminded us that in precolonial West Central Africa, customary laws governed free access to gold mining by landlord lineages and granted usufruct rights to mining and trading by selected strangers. Customary governance over minerals survived hegemonic control by centralized Sudanese states like fourteenth-century Mali, eighteenth-century Kong, and French colonial imposition in the late nineteenth to early twentieth centuries. Fierce resistance by lineage-based miners to intrusion by outsiders was driven not only by a need for subsistence livelihood but also by the worldview underpinning metals and ores. For example, "the mere presence of gold was essential at the cardinal ceremonies of baptism, circumcision or excision, marriage, and death, to tilt the balance between good and evil in the human life cycle" (457). Preserving the sacredness of the mining environment was crucial and included prohibiting entry by outsiders whose presence would pollute the moral and

16 CULTURE AND CONFLICTS IN SIERRA LEONE MINING

extractive environment and court disaster for communities. Only privileged strangers like Jula long-distance traders and advisors were exempt (Perinbam 1980). Indeed, Mansa Musa, ruler during the Empire of Mali's 'golden age' explained on his 1324 stay in Cairo en route to hajj in Mecca his reason for not assuming direct control of the goldfields but collecting tribute instead. Success with land-based production requires that only indigenes of a place (landlords) with established ancestral relationships with the spirits of the earth and bush manage natural resources (Canós-Donnay 2019). Perinbam (1988, 462) underscored the adaptive capacity and "resilience and the efficacy of a traditional system of mining and trade whose origins lie far back in the past of the western Sudan."

Important questions, therefore, that constitute the book's guiding posts are the following: How does the Sierra Leone government address the cultural differences in land management embedded in mineral commodity chains in policy and law? Is there an asymmetric transfer of cultural resources and norms from core and semi-peripheral countries to peripheral nations? Can this transfer be conceptualized as a culturally unequal exchange? Is "illicit" artisanal mining a form of cultural resistance against the impacts of incorporation on customary land rights? Do cultural resistance and cultural hybridity in Sierra Leone mining areas pose challenges to effective incorporation through mineral commodity chains? Can cultural resistance in the Sierra Leone mining sector trigger a development evolution that moves beyond capitalist extractivism toward new development trajectories that embody African cultural values? Or will the continuing marginalization of African cultural perspectives persist in the face of a capitalist global economy inexorably driving toward cultural universalism?

Methodology

To support my arguments, I traced the history of mining development in Sierra Leone and the evolution of policies and laws. I used information from archival, primary, and secondary sources, and a range of methods such as historical narrative analysis, legal analysis, and sociological/sociocultural analysis. I examined colonial and postcolonial Sierra Leone government policy and legislative documents, international government and nongovernment organizational reports, mining company reports and memoranda, narratives, newspapers, websites, scholarly publications. Major sources were the annual reports of the country's Mines and Geological Survey Departments dating back to 1921 and Sierra Leone colonial ordinances, postcolonial laws, and policies governing land and mining. Of particular interest were recently passed laws: The National Land Commission Act, 2022, and the Customary Land Rights

INTRODUCTION

Act, 2022. I particularly focused on how these documents acknowledged and addressed cultural differences in land management between customary and state approaches. I examined environmental and social impact assessment reports of two mining companies and include ethnographic data I collected as part of environmental consulting work in the rutile mining industry.

The findings from my Sierra Leone case study allow for generalizations based on the fact that other sub-Saharan African countries share comparable characteristics in their mining sectors. These include, for instance, national policy and legal reforms strongly influenced by colonial histories, landlord–stranger relationships, and international institutions like the World Bank that encourage significant FDI and favor capital-intensive mining by foreign multinationals.

Chapter 2

SIERRA LEONE'S GLOBAL INCORPORATION THROUGH MINING

> Historically, people throughout western Africa believed that smiths possessed redoubtable skills and powers. Only they knew the secrets of iron making and could secure the permission of the spirits of land, water, and forest to mine ores; only they could fell appropriate trees for charcoal making; and only they could invoke the spirits' cooperation in the smelting and forging of iron. Successful ironworking required the application of the smiths' considerable technological expertise, together with unremitting attention to requisite rituals. (Brooks 2003, 30)

Often when people think of Sierra Leone and mining, the first thought that comes to mind is conflict or blood diamonds. But there is much more than diamonds. The focus has been on diamond mining and the relationship with the warring factions of the large-scale Revolutionary United Front of Sierra Leone (RUF/SL) "blood diamond" war, 1991–2001, and its aftermath (Abdullah 2004; Fanthorpe and Maconachie 2010; Fanthorpe 2001; Jackson 2006; King 2007; Rashid 2004; Richards 2005). Researchers have analyzed the blood diamond war using a variety of conceptual frameworks such as the political economy (Hirsch 2001), the role of disenfranchised rural and urban youth, the so-called lumpen, as illegal diamond miners, and subsequently fighters in the RUF/SL war (Rashid 2004) greed, grievance, and governance (e.g., Bøås 2014; Frost 2012; Peters 2011). Others have written about the marginalization of youth within a gerontocratic system of traditional governance (Richards 2002) and the resource curse and actor–network theory (Wilson 2013). However, other minerals also played a role early on in Sierra Leone's global incorporation process and this continues today. Some minerals like iron ore and gold were mined by local people using artisanal methods of extraction for centuries (Goucher 1981; Wilson and Marmo 1958). I go beyond diamonds to address conflicts in other mineral extraction environments and in particular to highlight persistent low-level and smaller-scale conflicts that periodically turn violent.

Indigenous Artisanal Mining

Seventy percent of the Sierra Leone landmass contains mineral-rich basement rocks of the West African craton and supracrustal greenstone formations. A dense drainage network eroded and deposited alluvial deposits of minerals from the underlying rocks. Under the humid tropical climate, weathered and lateritic deposits also occur. Minerals include diamonds, gold, iron ore, chromium, columbite-tantalite, rutile, zircon, ilmenite, monazite, pyrochlore, bauxite, rare earth, sulfides of molybdenum, copper, zinc, lead, and iron as well as minor mineralizations of nickel, tin, vanadium, and cobalt. Figure 2.1 shows

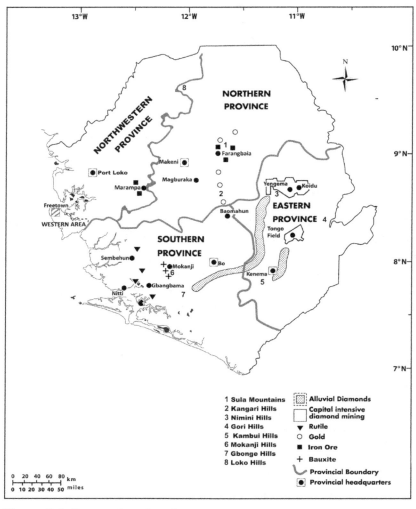

Figure 2.1 Some major mineral occurrences.

SIERRA LEONE'S GLOBAL INCORPORATION THROUGH MINING 21

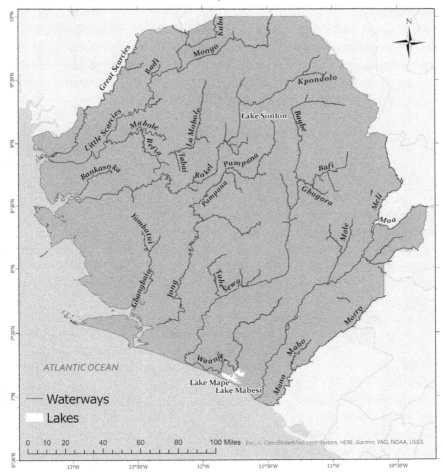

Figure 2.2 Sierra Leone waterways and lakes.

the location of some main mineral occurrences and Figure 2.2 shows the major river systems in the country.

In 1936, the Acting Chief Inspector of Mines K. E. Heesom and John Dudley Pollett, Assistant Geologist in the colonial Sierra Leone Geological and Mines Department, took an overland trip from Sierra Leone to neighboring Guinea. In the department's annual report, they documented seeing "native

22   CULTURE AND CONFLICTS IN SIERRA LEONE MINING

alluvial gold workings [...] an entirely native industry [where] some 25,000 are engaged" (Govt. of Sierra Leone 1937, 4, 7). What was not reflected in this record was that not everyone present at the mine site was involved in the physical extraction of minerals. Traditional or native artisanal mining is a multifaceted community activity. Other participants include financiers to miners, chiefs, and village elders as repositories of local knowledge on family land boundaries and rights, religious leaders offering prayers and sacrifices for productive mining, petty traders selling food and other necessities to miners, and casual observers. Since the introduction of external mining in the colonial period, state-employed Mine Wardens and Mine Monitoring Officers may be present at mine sites.

Artisanal mining and processing of minerals, such as gold and iron ore, are centuries-old, complementary livelihoods to subsistence farming and trade in Sierra Leone and West Africa, more broadly. Historically, the blacksmith is an essential patron in traditional Western African societies and a member of power associations. Blacksmiths prospected for mineral ores and produced iron tools on which the livelihoods of subsistence agricultural communities depended. They also made weapons for game hunting and for the many trade and resource wars characteristic of earlier times. Some crafted gold and silver jewelry. Typical smith clans of West Africa are Mandinka (Mandingo) speakers of Mande stock including Camara (Kamara), Kante (Conteh), and Koroma (Brooks 2003).

The landlord–stranger institution governs customary artisanal mining as a subsistence livelihood at the local level of the chiefdom in Sierra Leone. The chief and community elders in collaboration with landlord-indigene families disburse land for use by strangers. Strangers must have a landlord to act as their guardian and ensure they comply with the rules and customs of the chiefdom. The landlord takes responsibility for their behavior and receives an annual customary gift in cash and kind (Abraham and Gaima, 1996; Dorjahn and Fyfe 1966). The customary gift called *greeting kola* or *shakehand* is "a symbolic acknowledgment of the chief's jurisdiction and a formal indication by the stranger that he is prepared to respect and abide by the laws and customs of the chiefdom" (Renner-Thomas 2010, 172). In post-conflict Sierra Leone following the RUF/SL war period, strangers in various parts of the country include refugees, ex-combatants, and internally displaced people (Unruh 2008).

The Sierra Leone state officially recognizes the institution as a legitimate customary form of land tenancy in the National Land Policy (NLP) despite continuous impacts on its norms by the state development agenda (Govt. of Sierra Leone 2015c). Power associations in Sierra Leone that bolster the institution include *Poro, Wunde,* and *Gbangbani* for men and *Sande* or *Bondo/u* for women. Bush sites, forests, water bodies, and sacred shrines are integral to managing native land titles, subsistence livelihoods, intangible heritage practices, and community cultural sustainability (Abraham and Gaima 1996; Lebbie and Freudenberger 1996).

Sierra Leone is part of the long history of West African artisanal mining and trade in gold. The Mali Empire built on gold extended southeasterly into northern Sierra Leone in the fourteenth century (Canós-Donnay 2019). Gold deposits occur in many regions of Sierra Leone, and ancient mining sites include Lake Sonfon in the Sula Mountains in the north of the country. Artifacts like bored stones or *kwes* and stone picks found in West Africa, including Sierra Leone, are associated with such historic mining activity. Archaeologists found these artifacts among gold- and diamond-rich deposits in the highland region of southeastern Sierra Leone in the Kono District (Atherton 1972, 266, 1980; Goucher 1981).

Before nation-state boundaries in West Africa, the Julas or Maraka of the Mandingo ethnicity organized trading networks and commercial partnerships around the informal artisanal gold industry in the region. These long-distance traders were, and remain, investors and financiers who often welcome strangers to local communities. They sometimes participate in the exploitation of minerals, including the spread of gold mining techniques such as shallow underground mining in vertical Malian pits or *damas*. In the traditional African worldview, gold mining is not solely about economic efficiency to increase production as it is in the Western concept. It is guided by established social relationships, as discussed earlier. Gold mining and jewelry making remain meaningful traditional livelihoods, and Julas still finances women gold miners, in Sierra Leone (Govt. of Sierra Leone 2020).

The traditional Mande–Jula system of extraction, financing, and informal trading systems and the landlord–stranger institution managed artisanal mining. Women customarily pan for gold or sell food and goods at mine sites. Gold mining, in particular, helped to support daily life in rural communities where the mineral occurs. There was the understanding that miners would pay their Jula financiers in gold extracted and give them priority in buying any surplus. Landowners of the mine site receive a portion, too. In the minds of strangers and landlord-indigenes, maintaining good social relations around traditional livelihoods is as important as business profits. Due to the migratory nature of artisanal mining, one might be a host landlord on any given day and a stranger on another. Such reciprocal arrangements often extend to the farming season when stranger miners offer their labor on farms of landlord-indigenes for a share in the rice harvest (Panella 2010; Pipjers 2014).

24   CULTURE AND CONFLICTS IN SIERRA LEONE MINING

Financiers, locally called supporters in Sierra Leone, might also be mining license owners. They provide equipment, food, monetary loans, and stipends to the tributers who do the physical work. The premier mining law defined a tributer as "a person who directly or indirectly is permitted to win minerals receiving in return for the minerals so won remuneration paid directly or indirectly by the person who permitted him to win the minerals" (Govt. of Sierra Leone 2009). Supporters share a percentage of the value of any minerals found with the tributers rather than paying wages. In an alternative arrangement, *Gado*, self-funded groups of artisanal miners frequently comprising landlord-indigenes and strangers including traders form informal business relationships. They jointly fund mining operations and then divide the winnings into equal proportions (D'Angelo 2018). The Sierra Leone colonial government adopted the tributer system in the alluvial gold and diamond mining schemes initiated in the 1940s and 1950s, respectively.

In addition to gold, inhabitants in the area that is present-day Sierra Leone, possibly as early as AD 800 (CE), worked iron ore (Goucher 1981; Kaplan et al. 1976). Archaeologists discovered prehistoric iron tools, smelting slag, and ancient kilns in territory inhabited by the Kuluntuba Limba of Mande stock, believed to be the oldest inhabitants of Sierra Leone (Abraham and Gaiama 1996; Atherton 1972, 1980). There was trade in iron-worked goods in the fifteenth century between Sierra Leoneans and Portuguese explorers (Goucher 1981; Kaplan et al. 1976). Communities still practice this centuries-old craft of blacksmithing, manufacturing farming implements like hoes and cutlasses for subsistence agricultural communities. Blacksmiths' sacred bush sites and shrines for ceremonial rituals are found in Sierra Leone (Conteh 2009). In precolonial times, blacksmiths also made weapons for hunting and warfare, but at one point during the colonial period, the government banned production "in the interest of peace" (Fowler-Lunn 1938, 94).

In 1848, George E. Thompson, a missionary with the American Missionary Association, documented in detail seeing iron smelting at Lavannah village in southwestern Sierra Leone. He emphasized that the mode of smelting using charcoal was prevalent throughout the Mendi (Mende) country (Thompson 1969). Thomas Joshua Alldridge, District Commissioner in the Crown Colony of Sierra Leone, wrote in 1910 of a mountain south of the headquarters town of Bo called *Gai-in-giyeh* or Blacksmith's head by locals "so called because this mountain is stated to be full of ironstone, which was formerly worked." Alldridge was impressed by War Chief Kai-Lundu of Pendembu "holding two bright spears of native iron that glistened in the sun like silver." He also recorded that experienced Mende blacksmiths worked on the construction of the Sierra Leone Government Railway that started in 1896 (Alldridge 1910, 133, 178, 172).

European geologists carrying out mineral exploration in colonial Sierra Leone in the early twentieth century encountered ancient iron workings and smelters. They consistently documented the importance of a historical local and indigenous iron industry. Frank Dixey, a Director of the Sierra Leone Geological Survey (SLGS), wrote that iron ores in the northeastern Kono District were significant enough "[...] to be exploited by the people of the country for the local iron industry, which was formerly much more important than it is at present" (Govt. of Sierra Leone 1921, 17). Geologists N. W. Wilson and Vladi Marmo documented that "Old slag heaps near the handful of villages in the Sula Mountains testify that Africans have been smelting the lateritic ironstones for many years, possibly for many centuries. A particularly big heap is just north of the Kurumanto village on the path to Kunya" (Wilson and Marmo 1958, 66). The first Mineral Ordinance of 1927 recognized that iron ore extraction and processing was a customary livelihood and permitted locals to continue except within lands under a mining lease or right (The Sierra Leone Web 2023).

I share these examples to highlight the fact that there was a robust precolonial indigenous mining industry in Sierra Leone. Iron ore mine leases such as the African Minerals Ltd. (AML) lease coincide with historic indigenous mine sites. Figure 2.3 is an iron smelter from Sierra Leone of the earliest known style, the bloomery taken from a postcard by Litherland, Canning and Ashforth circa 1912–1914.

Mining in the Colonial and Postcolonial Eras

Gold mined artisanally using the traditional system was an important trade item with Europe in the nineteenth century. Zachary Macaulay, the first governor of the Colony of Sierra Leone, then Sierra Leone Company secretary, later established the transnational firm, Macaulay and Babington. The firm operated from 1807 to 1827, trading gold and other commodities (Akiwumi 2006; Metcalfe 1964). An 1822 expedition made by Dr. Obrien and Captain Laing into the interior of Sierra Leone and Guinea reached Boree and Kan Kan in present-day Guinea described as "the great gold countries in this part of Africa" (George 1968, 380). In a government trade report for the 10 years between 1854 and 1863, the value of gold exported from Sierra Leone ranged from a minimum of UK pounds 3610 in 1863 to a maximum of UK pounds 43,542 in 1860 (IUP 1968). Gold featured prominently in The Sierra Leone Protectorate Proclamation of 1897, which gave the Queen of England mining rights for gold, precious stones, and other minerals (Reeck 1976, 38).

Figure 2.3 Historic iron smelting furnace circa 1912–1914.

Sierra Leone's full-scale incorporation into the economic world system through mining began in the early twentieth century when demand for minerals on the global market increased (Akiwumi 2012). As early as 1910, the Imperial Institute analyzed rocks from the Freetown peninsula and found they contained metals like nickel, chromium, and titanium. Geologists collected soapstone (steatite) samples for the Great Britain Ministry of Munitions in 1917. Great Britain's munition Minister Winston L. S. Churchill later authorized geological and mineral surveys in that nation's African colonies for valuable minerals needed in Britain's manufacturing and military industries. Under the program, Second Lieutenant Frank Dixey arrived in Sierra Leone in 1918 as a government geologist assigned to conduct geological mapping. In 1919, Great Britain established an official SLGS.

Between 1918 and 1921, Dixey prepared a geomorphological map and discovered some vital mineral deposits (Dunham 1983; Govt. of Sierra Leone

1921, 1929). Dixey's work showed promising results, recording the presence of asbestos, graphite, monazite, zircon, garnet, and topaz (Govt. of Sierra Leone 1921, 18–22). The colonial administration in Sierra Leone gave top priority to mineral exploration, and the geological survey and mines department worked closely with the government of Great Britain, prospective British mining companies, and numerous scientific research institutions. For example, in 1921, the Powell Duffryn Steam Coal Company Ltd. of Aberdare, South Wales, helped the survey analyze clays for brick-making potential. The survey expressed outstanding indebtedness to the company (Govt. of Sierra Leone 1921, 15).

The British government sent Major Norman Junner, an experienced geologist from the Gold Coast Geological Survey (GCGS), to head the SLGS between 1926 and 1930. Junner identified and reported alluvial platinum and lignite on the Freetown Peninsula or Western Area, extensive and commercially exploitable iron ore deposits, alluvial gold and platinum in the Tonkolili District, and chromite in the Southern Province. Later, Junner and his assistant John Dudley Pollett found diamonds in the Kono District (Govt. of Sierra Leone 1930, 1932; The African World 1937). More surveys over time revealed base metals, bauxite, chromium, columbite-tantalite, copper, radioactive, and rare-earth minerals and titanium-bearing rutile and ilmenite (Govt. of Sierra Leone 1960). By 1928, the colonial government had granted 30 prospecting rights to foreign mining concerns with more applications waiting to be approved, especially exclusive prospecting rights for gold (Govt. of Sierra Leone 1929). Detailed geological fieldwork continued to reveal the extent and distribution of minerals.

There was much excitement by the Sierra Leone colonial government over Junner's so-called discovery of the iron ore deposits at Tonkolili. Annual reports of the geological and mines departments used exuberant terms to describe the deposits. For example, "[...] the magnitude and potentialities of these deposits [...]" and the "[...] immense deposit of really high grade" (Govt. of Sierra Leone 1934, 12). The preliminary estimate of available ore was approximately 74,000,000 tons. However, the report stated that "this figure is probably a conservative one. The geological evidence indicated that the ores are likely to extend to a much greater depth than 50 feet from the surface" (Govt. of Sierra Leone 1932, 4). The colonial government assigned Katherine Fowler-Lunn, an American geologist working for Maroc Co. Ltd., a gold mining company, to map the Tonkolili deposit. It was a rarity at the time to have a female geologist working in a male-dominated field, more so within a colonial administrative framework in an African country. She corroborated previous assessments: "The deposits are of unusual interest geologically, and in size represent one of the great iron ore reserves of the world" (Govt. of Sierra Leone 1932, 13).

28   CULTURE AND CONFLICTS IN SIERRA LEONE MINING

Many British scientific institutions supported the work of the survey by analyzing rock and soil specimens in their laboratories. These included the Atomic Energy Division under Great Britain's Ministry of Supply, Geochemical Prospecting Research Centre, Imperial College of Science and Technology, London; the Imperial Institute, Royal School of Mines, University College Cardiff, Colonial Development and Welfare (CDW) Schemes, and the Mineral Resources Division of Overseas Geological Surveys. The SLGS sometimes paid for these services, such as Imperial College of Science and Technology (Govt. of Sierra Leone 1930, 17; see Acknowledgments section). Doctoral students at British universities helped with field surveys and produced dissertations on Sierra Leone mineral exploration. Two examples from the Department of Mining Geology, Imperial College, University of London were Regional Geochemical Reconnaissance in the Northern and Southern Sections of the Sula Mountains Schist Belt, Sierra Leone (James 1965) and Geochemical prospecting studies in Sierra Leone (Mather 1959). Great Britain promoted the increasing importance of minerals from Sierra Leone with an exhibit at the Empire Mineral Exhibition hosted by the Imperial Institute in 1931 (Govt. of Sierra Leone 1932, 1).

Successful outcomes of Churchill's initiative, namely the discovery of strategic and economic minerals in British colonies, led to the enactment of the CDW Act of 1929. The purpose was to facilitate the exploitation of mineral deposits in colonies for export to Great Britain and its allies. The Act provided low-interest loans to British companies interested in exploiting mineral resources in territories such as Sierra Leone. Industrial diamonds and iron ore were important for the British armament industry at the time. Colonies would get revenue from royalties and taxation. In 1929, a dispatch C.O. 267/627/9292JL dated August 10, 1929 to all the Colonial Governors from Lord Passfield, Secretary of State for the Colonies, made clear the general British government policy behind the Act:

> [...] to achieve the twofold objects of assisting the economic development of the Colonial Empire by the promotion of commerce with and industry in this country, and reducing unemployment in the United Kingdom. (cited in Hoogvelt and Tinker 1978, 70)

The CDW Act only permitted colonial governments to submit applications for grants and loans from the fund, which a Colonial Development Advisory Committee would then review. While the act was under discussion, the Governor representing Her Majesty's government in Sierra Leone expressed reservations about the government financing private sector companies. Notwithstanding his concern, the powerful hand of business interests took precedence. The Colonial Development Fund (CDF) soon began to disburse loans to mining projects with the potential to make a profit. Three powerful business entities jointly obtained a concession for iron ore deposits in northern Sierra Leone in 1929: the Northern Mercantile and Investment Corporation (NMIC), United Africa Company (UAC), a subsidiary of Lever Brothers, now Unilever, and the African and Eastern Trading Corporation (AETC). The Sierra Leone colonial government had no laws and regulations specifically for mining at the time. So, the group obtained a prospecting license under the Concessions Ordinance of 1924, which covered land uses, more broadly. In 1927, the colonial government passed an ordinance specific to minerals and mining. Meanwhile, the business partners worked with the Crown Agents for the colonies on an application for a loan from the CDW fund. The loan of UK Pounds 500,000 was submitted on behalf of the Sierra Leone Colony to develop the deposits. In reality, there was little input from the colony and the application process started before the CDW Act officially passed. The advisory committee approved the loan as soon as the act passed. Subsequently, the partners registered the Sierra Leone Development Company (SLDC) Ltd. in England under the Companies Act in 1929 to work the deposits (Segkoma 1986).

The iron ore deposits occurred inland and around the village of Marampa in Port Loko District, Northwestern Province. The CDW funding was primarily to fund the construction of the railway that would transport the iron ore from Marampa to the Sierra Leone River for loading onto ships bound for Europe at the Port of Pepel. The SLDC signed the Tonkolili Agreement in 1931, a Special Exclusive Prospecting License (SEPL) for iron ore and any other minerals found in the Tonkolili area. The SEPL also permitted an extension of the railway line from Marampa to the proposed mine site at Farangbaia and rights to any lands the company required for this infrastructure for 999 years! (Sierra Leone Web 2023).

The Minerals Ordinance 1927 vested all land and mineral resources in the Crown and regulated the right to explore, extract, and process minerals and any other related purposes. The colonial government amended the ordinance numerous times in response to the evolving nature of the mineral industry, more mineral discoveries, and an increasing need for land, water, and revenue. For example, continuous geological mapping and mineral exploration revealed the interrelationship between river and groundwater systems and mineral deposits. This connection dictated that mineral rights were essentially water rights, so the colonial government added water appropriation to the mining ordinance. The Minerals (Amendment) Ordinance (No. 17 of 1932), therefore, declared: "the entire property in all minerals and of all rivers and watercourses resides in the Crown." The

30   CULTURE AND CONFLICTS IN SIERRA LEONE MINING

amendment was one of two described as "undoubtedly the most important legislation connected with mining because it allowed the governor to approve special agreements granting water rights to individual mining companies" (Govt. of Sierra Leone 1934, 12). Water rights, in general, embodied the right to dredge river courses. The Mineral (Amendment) Ordinance (No. 30 of 1938) explicitly "provided for the dredging for minerals in rivers, streams, and watercourses" (Wohlwend 1979).

With prospecting and exploitation of other minerals, additional ordinances, regulations, and orders were needed to facilitate the mining operations. The government granted SEPLs, leases, and customized legal agreements for individual companies. These customized agreements made at the Governor's discretion typically exempted those companies from adhering to provisions in the overarching Minerals Ordinance (Govt. of Sierra Leone 1932). I give some examples below. The Governor first exercised this right with the passage of the Rokel River Water Rights Agreement (Ratification) Ordinance (No. 31 of 1938) to benefit the SLDC mining iron ore at Marampa. The ordinance gave the company the "exclusive and preferential right to the use of the Rokel River waters" for 89 years. The company could construct a pumping station and an accompanying pipeline system on the river and pump out as much water as needed for the mining process.

The Sierra Leone Selection Trust (SLST), a subsidiary of the Consolidated African Selection Trust (CAST), and Maroc Co. Ltd. were the first foreign companies to extract alluvial deposits of diamonds and gold, respectively, starting in the 1930s. The agreements governing their extraction contained extensive land and water rights. The first SLST lease in 1932 covered the entire country for 99 years. The colonial government passed additional water legislation for the company in 1935 permitting mining in the lower reaches of the Moa and Sewa Rivers in the Kenema, Bo, Bonthe, and Pujehun Districts. Through an Order in Council, the Rivers Sewa and Moa Closed Areas to Prospecting Order (No. 24 of 12 December 1935), the government designated diamond-rich lands along the river as closed areas. A revised diamond agreement in the 1950s between the SLST and the government reduced the lease to a 780 square kilometers (310 square miles) zone that included the most diamond-rich ground, such as Tongo Field. However, SLST still retained prospecting rights over the whole country (Govt. of Sierra Leone 1936; van der Laan 1965, 44). Maroc Ltd. and other gold mining concerns obtained rights in the Rokel and Pampana River basins draining the Sula Mountains–Kangari Hills schist belt.

There was interest in other minerals too. The government continued collaboration with Great Britain relying on the scientific and technical expertise within British research institutions and mining companies to evaluate mineral resources, demarcate leases, and craft special agreements. For example, the SLGS invited Dr. J. R. F. Joyce, a renowned mining geologist employed by British Titans Products (BTP) Company Ltd., to evaluate titanium mineral deposits in southwestern Sierra Leone. The BTP subsequently obtained a Special Exclusive Prospecting License. In 1959, the government passed the Titanium Minerals Agreement to develop and extract deposits. The ordinance gave extensive water rights for dredge mining operations. This arrangement of companies seeking to mine deposits also doing the mineral exploration and ore evaluation was a matter of concern to observers like the United Nations Economic Commission for Africa (UNECA). Further, the data gathered was not routinely shared with the SLGS. The Sierra Leone government revised the 1959 special agreement in 1972, 1989, and 2002 as the Sierra Rutile Agreement (Govt. of Sierra Leone 2002; UNESC-ECA 1968a, 1968b; UNECA 1969).

The government granted the first Bauxite Mineral Prospecting and Mining Agreement to Swiss Aluminium Ltd. (now Alusuisse-Lonza Holding Ltd.) and the locally incorporated subsidiary Sierra Leone Ore and Metal Company Ltd. on October 31, 1961. The agreement was revised in 1976, 1980, 1987, and 1992 (Govt. of Sierra Leone 1992). There are persistent clauses in all versions of the special agreements for bauxite, rutile, and diamonds. For example, the company within or outside its mining lease area can cut down trees and clear land; dig, widen, and deepen river and stream channels and watercourses; use water from any natural water course and return wastewater with washing spoils back to the source. However, the water should not be discharged if it contains poisonous or noxious substances. The titanium agreement allows diverting water bodies outside the lease and building dams to create dredge ponds for operations.

In addition to acquiring mineral-bearing lands, the special agreements give additional lands for ancillary purposes or provide the option to acquire more land as needed after operations start. For example, the Marampa Railway and Harbour Works Ordinance (No. 2 of 1931) allowed the SLDC to obtain additional lands for railway and harbor works. The company constructed a 33-km-long rail line between the mine site at Marampa and the seaport at Pepel. This rail line had a 1-m-wide gauge and was more efficient compared to the government line that transported people and farm products with a gauge width of 0.75 m (Lewis 1954).

The Minerals Ordinance of 1927 became the Revised Minerals Act of 1960, the Mines and Minerals Decree of 1994, the Mineral and Mines Act of 2009, and the current Mines and Minerals Development Act of 2021. Slight amendments were done in 1999 and 2004 and supplementary documents included the Mines and Minerals Operational Regulations, 2013 and the Mines

32 CULTURE AND CONFLICTS IN SIERRA LEONE MINING

and Minerals (Environment Protection) Regulations, 2013. Subsequent acts have increasingly emphasized more participation in the mining sector and economic benefits for Sierra Leoneans, environmental and social issues, community development, and health and safety for mineworkers and host community residents. However, a consistent colonial vestige in this primary mining law is that "All rights of ownership in and control of minerals in, under or upon any land in Sierra Leone and its continental shelf are vested in the Republic" (Govt. of Sierra Leone 2021).

Currently, a Minerals Advisory Board under the National Minerals Agency approves licenses and advises the Minister of Mines accordingly. For artisanal mining, the Director of Mines is responsible for allocating licenses. The Mining Cadastre Office registers mineral rights and rights applications detailing information on owners, minerals, and areas covered by leases and licenses. In 2019, the register showed 1487 active mining licenses for mineral exploration, large-scale, small-scale, and artisanal mining covering all drainage basins. There are nine special agreements granting concessions for large-scale mining as shown in Table 2.1. Other large-scale

Table 2.1 Current special agreements for large-scale mining.

Mining Company	Agreement	Mineral	District
Sierra Rutile Limited	Rutile Mining Agreement 2002	Rutile, ilmenite, zircon	Bonthe, Moyamba
Sierra Rutile Limited	Rutile Mining Agreement 2004 SRL Acquisition No. 3 Limited	Rutile, ilmenite, zircon	Bonthe, Moyamba
African Minerals Limited	Iron Ore Mining Agreement 2010	Iron ore	Tonkolili
Koidu Holdings SA	Diamonds Mining Agreement, 2010, 2012	Diamonds	Kono
London Mining Company Limited	Iron Ore Mining Agreement 2014, 2017	Iron ore	Port Loko
Tonguma Limited	Diamonds Gold Mining Agreement 2012	Diamonds, gold	Kono
Sierra Minerals Holdings	Bauxite Mining Agreement 2012	Bauxite	Moyamba
SL Mining Limited	Iron Ore Mining Agreement 2014, 2017	Iron ore	Port Loko
SierraMin Bauxite Limited	Bauxite Concession Agreement 2017	Bauxite	Port Loko

Source: EITI. 2021. Sierra Leone 2019 EITI report. https://eiti.org/countries/sierra-leone.

operators include African Railway and Port Services, Dayu Investment Ltd., H.M. Diamonds, Kingho Investment Co. (now Leone Rock Metal Group), Meya Mining (diamonds, gold, and associated minerals), and Sierra Diamonds Ltd. Some examples of medium-scale operations are Afro-Asia Mining Corp. Ltd. (ilmenite, rutile, zircon) and Xin Tai Mining Co. Ltd. (gold). In total, 36 companies contribute 10 percent or more to government revenue from the extractive industries.

Kingho Investment Company, a Chinese entity, took over the management of African Minerals Ltd.'s iron ore concession in the Tonkolili District. The company changed its name to Leone Rock Metal Group in 2021 with Kingho Mining Company and Kingho Railway and Port Company as subsidiaries. They collectively operated the open pit mine, a 192-km railway and a port at Pepel in northwest Sierra Leone. However, in January 2023, the Sierra Leone government signed a lease agreement with ARISE Integrated Industrial Platforms Ltd. for the Pepel Port and Pepel—Tonkolili Railway Development, Expansion, and Management project. Wongor Investment and Mining Corp. Ltd., another Chinese concern, runs the first large-scale industrial-scale gold mine at Komahun, Nimikoro chiefdom in Kono District. Around 70,000 miners are active in the artisanal sector and women make up 18%. However, some 900,000 people benefit from mining and other economic opportunities generated by the industry. A 2020 government study identified 700 operating mine sites for diamonds (485), gold (200), and coltan (15) (EITI 2021; Remoe 2023; Thomas 2023).

Since the beginning of mining by foreign companies, Chiefdom Councils (former Tribal Authorities) as custodians of the community lands participated in transactions with companies and the state through cooptation or coercion. The District Officer (former District Commissioner) represents the government. The concept of land as a marketable commodity or subject to a long-term lease as stated in laws is problematic for traditional authority. The practice of a long-term lease is contrary to customary land management. As such, traditional authorities cannot negotiate effectively for their communities to benefit fairly from surface rents and royalties. For example, the Marampa Tribal Authorities received only UK Pounds 250 and an annual royalty amount of UK Pounds 12 for the land given up to SLDC (DELCO) in 1929 for iron ore extraction. The company made 250 times more than the UK Pounds 250 within five years of obtaining the concession. Further, the SLDC paid no profit taxes until 1939 when the Sierra Leone colonial government levied a meager amount of five percent (Hoogvelt and Tinker 1978; Segkoma 1986).

Once land is given, foreign companies function as more or less independent establishments. They depend on capital, professional manpower, machinery,

34   CULTURE AND CONFLICTS IN SIERRA LEONE MINING

and supplies from abroad and rely on global markets. The length of extractive operations is dependent on world market prices for specific minerals. Communities in mining areas receive revenue generated from company operations as a portion of national government expenditure. Recently reformed mining laws require companies to interact with host communities through community development initiatives and corporate social responsibility (CSR) programs and procure a certain amount of goods, locally (Cleeve 1997; Wilson 2015; Govt. of Sierra Leone 2021).

The granting of leases to mining companies allowed nontraditional forms of land management to appropriate customary lands and waters and consequently impact local livelihoods like farming and fishing. Prospecting and extraction affect communities and their ecological resource base and water sources. Villages are typically located near rivers, streams, or swamps for access to domestic water supply, fishing, and other riparian activities. Consequently, livelihoods including traditional artisanal mining struggle to survive at the margins of leases. To compound this problem, a 1931 amendment to the Mineral Ordinance introduced the notion of "unlawful possession of minerals" and the infliction of heavy penalties for any violation (Govt. of Sierra Leone 1934, 13). All these changes instigated conflicts and cultural resistance by landlord-indigene communities. Thus, ordinances to appropriate minerals, land, and water necessitated more ordinances to manage related cultural conflicts. Chapter 3 shows how the cultural disputes over land use, including mining, greatly influenced the formulation and revisions of policies and laws.

Chapter 3

CULTURAL DIFFERENCE: POLICY AND LEGISLATIVE DILEMMAS

This is the price paid for winning the country's wealth. To the European mine manager—himself often of working-class origin—it seems no special problem. As he sees matters, if the country is to get on, if things are to be made "efficient", then the tribal system with its traditional outlook on land and obligation to the community, must go. (Lewis 1954, 200)

Addressing cultural conflict over land management in ordinances dates back to the nineteenth-century timber trade in Sierra Leone. Traders who rampantly exploited forest resources were strangers, Europeans, and Creole descendants of formerly enslaved people resettled in the Colony of Sierra Leone centered around Freetown. The Creoles although ethnic African were classified by the government as British subjects. As wealthy and influential strangers, they often appropriated landlord-indigenes' customary rights and authority over land management. Chiefs responded to this injustice in traditional ways by imposing *poro* sanctions that prohibited laborers from, for instance, moving timber logs. Great Britain's response was to establish the Sierra Leone Protectorate by Ordinance to control trade in valuable commodities like timber and to acquire additional lands for extraction (Fyfe 1962).

John Hargreaves (1956, 70) explained that "the most drastic intervention from London with respect to the Protectorate Ordinance of 1897 was on the lands question." One of its provisions overtly prohibited the use of poro sanctions to govern resources, a method that had been used for centuries. Another provision vested all mineral rights in the Crown. Further, under the ordinance, the Governor had the power to grant land rights to non-natives or strangers. In contrast, customary law states that land which comprises "the surface soil and things found naturally under, on or above the surface, such as minerals and wild plants and trees. Man-made structures and cultivated crops are distinct from the land itself. The land is inalienable. Heads of landlord-indigene families are responsible for distributing any

36   CULTURE AND CONFLICTS IN SIERRA LEONE MINING

benefits accruing from land which in mining lease areas include surface rent payments stipulated in statutory law" (Renner-Thomas 2010, 177).

Ordinances also allowed the Governor to dispose of perceived waste and uninhabited lands. The colonial narrative of the wastefulness of "the fallow wildernesses" everywhere in Sierra Leone (Alldridge 1910, 189) was inscribed in the Unoccupied Lands (Ascertainment of Title) Ordinance (No. 12 of 1911):

> All lands shall be deemed to be unoccupied lands when it is not proved by the person claiming the land that it has been beneficially used for 12 years, prior to the commencement of the ordinance. If lands marked out as unoccupied lands are not claimed they shall be deemed to be Crown land. (Great Britain Colonial Office 1949, 54)

This ordinance did not consider customary land practices and perceptions of unoccupied land. The notion of wasteland is not common under the traditional subsistence livelihood practices of shifting cultivation, hunting and gathering wild crops, and artisanal mining. For example, farming communities leave the land to fallow after several years of cultivation. In the historic past before population pressure on land, the fallow period could be up to 25 years for the tropical soils to adequately regenerate. So 12 years was somewhat arbitrary and showed a poor understanding of and disregard for customary land practices. Further, seemingly unoccupied or abandoned lands and unexploited forests often have deep cultural significance for communities as a "resonant and living memoryscape" inhabited by ancestral spirits. Trees and other features of the natural landscape "can be read as ruins ... as much as decaying, destroyed buildings" (Ferme 2000, 25). Some sites "might be places of explicit commemorative rituals" while others, with negative associations, are consciously left to be consumed by the forest in a process of so-called cultural forgetting. Whether actively used, or not, such sites become part of a community's mental landscape (Basu 2013, 122).

The Sierra Leone colonial state continued to impact the landlord–stranger institution as it modified elements of customary land management to accommodate new land uses. When the government amended The Protectorate Land Ordinance in 1927, it retained the provision prohibiting *poro* sanctions. The amendment empowered the colonial Provincial Commissioner and District Commissioner to override decisions on "any matters that have their origin in indigenous institutions such as *poro* laws, native rights or customs, ... land disputes." In addition, the ordinance exempted anyone employed in an industry like mining from customary obligations to chiefs under the landlord–stranger relationship. The Provinces Land Ordinance of 1933 replaced the Protectorate Ordinance and still exempted strangers

CULTURAL DIFFERENCE 37

employed in any industry from obligations to landlords. The term "non-native" was substituted for "stranger" (Renner-Thomas 2010, 12).

Following Independence in 1961, the District Officer and Provincial Secretary representing the national government still have the final say on land matters. However, they do consult with the Chiefdom Councils and landlord-indigene families owning land. Mining companies as non-natives in commercial enterprise pay rent to landholders and chiefs for lands leased in chiefdoms.

The expansion of the mining industry complicated the dilemma over state recognition of landlord-indigenes' rights to govern land in customary ways including managing strangers. The constant influx of people into mining areas seeking a variety of economic opportunities expanded the categories of strangers beyond traders, subsistence farmers, and artisanal miners. The multinational companies, as stranger establishments, hold a powerful position compared to their landlords in host mining communities through state laws. As international entities, they hire other strangers of different races, ethnicities, and nationalities as expatriates and Sierra Leonean mining professionals (administrators, chemists, engineers, geologists), security officers, and wage laborers. For example, strangers employed at Sierra Rutile Ltd. (SRL), a capital-intensive operation, over the years, have included Australian, American, British, Malaysian, Ghanaian, New Zealander, South African, and Sierra Leonean nationals. In doing so, companies generate other categories of strangers empowered and protected by mining laws. Table 3.1 compares an

Table 3.1 Changes to traditional sociopolitical structures caused by mining.

Traditional Social Hierarchy (administering subsistence livelihoods)	Restructured Social Hierarchy from Mining
Chiefs and Poro Council	MNC and mining company professional employees (expatriates, Sierra Leoneans) (strangers)
Core members of landholding lineages	
Dependents/Subjects (farm families)	Diamond dealers, financiers, license holders, smugglers
Immigrant farmers (strangers)	
	Immigrant wage labor, legal and illegal artisanal miners, retailers, service providers (strangers)
	Chiefs and Poro Council
	Core members of land holding lineages
	Dependents/Subjects (farm families). Refugees, ex-combatants, illegal diggers (strangers)

Source: Akiwumi 2014.

38   CULTURE AND CONFLICTS IN SIERRA LEONE MINING

old and new hierarchy in mining areas showing how other stranger groups have superseded landlord-indigenes. Control over land and the right to grant access to land is no longer the reality for Chiefdom Councils and landlord-indigenes in areas under a mining lease.

From a customary perspective, the Sierra Leone state in search of revenue from mining is implicit in stranger hierarchy creation in mining regions. However, mining laws require that companies pay surface rent to landholding families who are the landlord-indigenes in the extraction region. An example is the postcolonial Sierra Rutile Agreement of 2002, which requires the company, as a non-native stranger, leasing land in chiefdoms for mining to pay these dues (Govt. of Sierra Leone 2002).

In artisanal mining areas, historically dominant stranger groups who thrive in the industry include Lebanese, Syrians, Maraka (Mandingo), and Fula, who are long-term and deeply rooted immigrants in Sierra Leone. Migrants of various Sierra Leone ethnicities and foreign nationals from neighboring African countries also in-migrate. Dominant stranger groups are, typically, artisanal or small-scale mining license holders, mineral dealers (buyers), smugglers, or mining equipment retailers. License holders and dealers may also finance mining operations like other supporters. Less powerful strangers are the artisanal legal and illegal diggers and the service providers, for example, food sellers, shopkeepers, tailors, and bar and nightclub owners who cater to the burgeoning mining communities. With minerals such as gold, diamonds, coltan, and zircon, it is possible to participate in what reports of the Mines Department historically label as "illicit" mining. Such high-value minerals can be extracted with rudimentary methods and low-level technology, and easily be smuggled.

The colonial and postcolonial governments periodically privileged some stranger groups to facilitate mineral extraction and trade. Although there is historically an ambivalent relationship between Lebanese and Sierra Leoneans in business ventures, the former nevertheless dominated the gold and diamond industries as shown in Tables 3.2 and 3.3. They had access to capital for investment and were successful as license holders, traders, and smugglers. As such, they held a more privileged position as strangers compared to the Marakas. The annual reports of the mines department documented their business acumen and success as they began to dominate the industry (Govt of Sierra Leone 1948; Reno 1995; Sutherland 1977; van der Laan 1965). The Annual Report of the Mines Department for 1939 highlighted that "Syrian operators were taking full advantage of the tributer system" (Govt. of Sierra Leone 1939, 2).

Although tallied as African in the mines reports, Creoles were officially British subjects during the colonial era. African laborers were Sierra Leoneans of varied ethnicity. Table 3.2 shows that overall the number of Africans with

CULTURAL DIFFERENCE

Table 3.2 License holders in the gold mining industry and African labor, 1929–1944.

Year	No. of Companies & Syndicates			Mining License Holders		African Labor		
	Foreign Co.	Local Co.	Syndicates	European	Lebanese	African	Creole	Indigenous
1929	3	0	0					
1930	2	0	1	0	0	0	0	64
1931	2	1	0	0	0	0	0	n/a
1932	2	0	0	0	0	0	0	2362
1933	3	0	0	0	0	7	1	3395
1934	3	0	2	0	3	13	0	5782
1935	4	5	3	11	8	15	0	8401
1936	5	3	7	13	15	8	0	7946
1937	5	1	4	13	15	3	1	7830
1938	5	2	0	11	18	0	1	10509
1939	3	1	1	7	27	0	1	9913
1940	3	2	1	5	32	0	2	7445
1941	3	2	1	6	21	0	1	3314
1942	2	1	1	6	17	0	1	1235
1943	2	1	1	4	12	0	1	542
1944	2	1	1	3	8	0	0	142
Total	49	20	23	79	176	46	8	68,880

Source: Akiwumi 2014; Annual Reports of the Geological and Mines Department, 1929–1944.

40 CULTURE AND CONFLICTS IN SIERRA LEONE MINING

Table 3.3 Number of alluvial diamond dealers' licenses held by citizens and noncitizens, 1959–1971.

Year	Natives of Sierra Leone/Citizen	Non-natives/Noncitizen
1959	176	85
1960	209	127
1961	192	101
1962	95	74
1963	65	103
1964	70	122
1965	63	129
1966	48	116
1967	57	23
1968	65	115
1969	76	134
1970	47	127
1971	58	121
Total	1221	1377

Source: Akiwumi 2014; Govt. of Sierra Leone: Reports of the Mines Department, 1959–1971.

the financial resources to own mining licenses was very small. Few of these, moreover, had landlord claims to land in gold mining areas. Even when the government introduced the Alluvial Gold Mining Scheme (AGMS) by Ordinance in 1946 to encourage indigenous participation, foreigners and Lebanese largely financed such ventures. The government reports documented the fact that foreign financiers were actually behind the so-called native firms, defined as companies where "more than half of the share capital is held by natives of Sierra Leone" (Govt. of Sierra Leone 1961, 9).

Table 3.3 displays information for diamond dealer licenses from 1959 to 1971 recorded in the annual Mines Department reports. Unlike the 1934–1944 reports that gave a more detailed breakdown of the nationality of mining license holders, the license categories were collapsed into only two—citizens and noncitizens—thereby obfuscating who specifically held the licenses. As the table shows for 1963, noncitizens for the first time received more diamond dealer licenses than indigenous Sierra Leoneans. The Annual Report of the Mines Department for 1964 explained that these noncitizen dealers were mostly Lebanese who had greater access to finance and formed partnerships with other dealers, some of who were indigenous (Govt. of Sierra Leone 1966). The decline in 1967 of noncitizen licenses was due to the National Reformation Council (NRC) decree from the ruling

CULTURAL DIFFERENCE 41

military junta that was in power for one year. During this time, the national government took over issuing alluvial mining licenses from the chiefdom authorities (Zack-Williams 1995).

The Government Gold and Diamond Office (GGDO) documented in 2003 that the incentive of reduced license fees for Sierra Leonean citizens to participate in alluvial mining ventures still did not produce the intended outcomes. Citizens with little capital obtained licenses and continued to be financed by noncitizens. The GGDO annual report for 2003 reported some data on license holders. As an example, of 131 licensed diamond dealers, "93 were 'citizens' (although not all were necessarily indigenous Sierra Leoneans), 18 were noncitizens, and 20 were Economic Community of West African States (ECOWAS) nationals" (Partnership Canada Africa 2004, 15).

Ordinances and More Ordinances

Despite the semantics of categorizing, describing, or classifying various actors in Sierra Leone mining areas by the government, the fundamental issue is cultural. Mining occurs on the ancestral lands of landlord-indigenes, and strangers play a dominant role in the mineral commodity chain operations. I elaborate on the history of this categorization problem in colonial and postcolonial state policies and laws to foreground the cultural conflict dilemma. Illicit artisanal mining close to leases granted to foreign companies like Maroc Co. Ltd. (gold) and the SLST (diamonds) in the 1930s was the major driver of policies and laws specifically referencing the cultural notion of "strangers." However, some areas covered by leases were coincident with customary mining sites as I mentioned earlier, so the government had to rethink strategies to address the persistence of unwanted stranger activities. The government collaborated with companies to devise ordinances and associated orders/by-laws and rules. This was particularly the case for diamond exploitation as clearly articulated in official documents.

While the colonial government recognized that artisanal mining was a well-established traditional livelihood, local miners could not work the deposits within a lease granted to a foreign company. Under rules associated with the Minerals Ordinance of 1927, a mining company could "demarcate and enclose areas within its mining lease, forbid entry and/or search any entrants into these demarcated areas with the exception of authorized officials" (Govt. of Sierra Leone 1936, 8). Authorized officials included expatriate mine employees who were non-native strangers but not landlord community members. The SLST almost immediately after acquiring its lease had barracks and an office for a diamond protection police force built by 1935 to prevent theft (Govt. of Sierra Leone 1936, 6). An amendment to the Minerals

42 CULTURE AND CONFLICTS IN SIERRA LEONE MINING

Ordinance in 1931 defined "unlawful possession of minerals" and increased "penalties for their unlawful possession" (Govt. of Sierra Leone 1932, 26).

The main goal of the legislation was to control stranger movement, protect the SLST diamond lease against encroachment, and expel illicit miners categorized as strangers from mining districts and chiefdoms. Colonial ordinances included the Diamond Area Protection Ordinance first passed in 1933, The Aliens (Control in Special Areas) Ordinance, The Aliens (Expulsion) Ordinance, and The Immigration Restriction Ordinance of 1946. In addition, some orders associated with The Tribal Authorities Ordinance specifically targeted strangers in mining environments, for instance, The Tribal Authorities (Control/Restriction of Strangers in Kono District) Order and the Tribal Authorities (Control of Strangers in Chiefdoms) Order (Govt. of Sierra Leone 1937, 1961; Govt. of Sierra Leone, various years). In reality, not all strangers were artisanal miners nor did all miners operate illegally. Many strangers simply took advantage of other economic opportunities generated by the mining industry.

The rules associated with the Diamond Industry Protection Ordinance dealt: "chiefly with the residence of strangers in the district" (Govt. of Sierra Leone 1937, 9). This ordinance and others that followed often used derogatory language to describe illicit miners equated with strangers. For example, amendments to The Ordinance made in 1956 gave "new definitions of a 'stranger' and 'native of Sierra Leone'" and were "to effect removals and exclusions of undesirables from Diamond Protected Areas" (Govt. of Sierra Leone 1961, 7). The Aliens (Expulsion) Ordinance and The Aliens (Control in Special Areas) Ordinance similarly characterized artisanal miners as aliens, undesirables, and lawless elements carrying out illicit activities. Reports lamented the "menace of illicit mining" (Govt. of Sierra Leone 1955, 1960a, 7).

Periodic government-funded expulsion drives to evict strangers also used dramatic code names, some with negative connotations, Operation Parasite, Operation Digger, Operation Clean Spring, Operation Stranger 2, Exodus I and II, and Operation Clean Slate (D'Angelo 2022; Govt. of Sierra Leone 1958a; Harbottle 1976; van der Laan 1965). This approach fueled the illicit narrative. The "customary stranger" became synonymous with the "statutory alien," an illustration of the cultural hybridity and cultural imperialism of the incorporation process through commodity chains.

To complicate things further, there were ambiguities and contradictions between the many legal instruments (ordinances and related orders/by-laws and rules) addressing strangers in the context of the mining industry. The frequent redefinition of a stranger to address the continuing illicit mining dilemma was a culturally complex problem in itself. Early on, The Diamond

CULTURAL DIFFERENCE   43

Industry Protection Ordinance defined a stranger as "any person other than a native of the Protectorate." This meant anyone from any district in the Sierra Leone Protectorate, even if of a different ethnicity, was not a stranger in Kono District. However, amendments to the ordinance in 1954 as part of the government renegotiating a new diamond agreement with SLST defined a "stranger" as "any person in an area declared to be a diamond protection area, who according to native law and custom does not belong to that District" (Daily Mail 1954). Other Africans from neighboring countries were "native strangers" or "native foreigners" as defined by the Immigration Restriction Ordinance (Colonial Office 1947). Europeans were "non-natives" as were Creoles from Freetown (The Colony) and some Lebanese and Syrians as British subjects. Currently, the terms citizens and noncitizens and foreigners or foreign nationals are commonly used.

Operation Parasite, the largest mass deportation of an estimated 45,000 "native foreigners" from diamond mining areas in the Kono, Kenema, and Bo Districts, occurred in 1956. Sierra Leone Governor Maurice Dorman threatened to use police and military force if needed. Those targeted were from African countries such as Guinea, Liberia, Mali, and Senegal. The expulsion program started on October 31, 1956. It involved international intervention by France to curtail illicit activities of French West African colonial subjects in neighboring Guinea. Sekou Toure and Saifoulaye Diallo, representatives from the colony of Guinea in the French parliament, facilitated the negotiations with Dorman (Colonial Office 1958, 6). The Governor politicized the stranger-as-illicit-miner narrative to further rile up anti-stranger feelings among landlord-indigenes (D'Angelo 2022). There was much public discourse during the period leading up to the start of the expulsion drive. The Sierra Leone *Daily Mail* newspaper in October 1956 carried several articles for and against the issue of strangers in mining areas. Titles included "Governor's Guiding Hand," "Strangers Are Crowding Us Out: Paul Dunbar Tells of Kono Problem," and "LegCo Passes Bill to Eject 'Strangers': Dunbar Warns against Armed Resistance." Paul Dunbar was a well-known Kono leader (Daily Mail 1956a, 1956b, 1956c).

Following Operation Parasite, the annual report of the Mines Department opined:

It is slow business to break up the illicit mining and dealing which has been well entrenched for some time. A great help however was His Excellency the Governor's firm action in expelling the "strangers" in November who represented a large part of those engaged in illicit mining. (Govt. of Sierra Leone 1958a, 1)

44　　CULTURE AND CONFLICTS IN SIERRA LEONE MINING

This seeming optimism that the problem was somewhat under control was short lived. With the departure of "native foreigners," more Sierra Leone Protectorate natives began moving into Kono District to participate in the activity. In February 1957, some three months after Operation Parasite, the so-called Kono Disturbances occurred. Some 300 illicit miners mainly from the Temne ethnic group encroaching on the SLST lease attacked a police patrol and later the police station near Yomadu. Another attack of an even larger scale occurred later in the year which the mines department reported:

> Late in August, there was a sudden large incursion of several thousands of illicit miners into the areas of the Sierra Leone Selection Trust resulting in considerable disorder and damage to one of the Company's pan plants. Reinforcement of police and military were moved into the area and order was quickly restored. (Govt. of Sierra Leone 1959, 4)

The government provided an Auxiliary Police Force and troops to help the SLST's Diamond Protection Force secure the lease areas and the company constructed barracks to house them (Govt. of Sierra Leone 1959, 6). There was also some action against smugglers in 1957 when the colonial government deported five Lebanese smugglers (van der Laan 1965, 24).

In response to the pervasive problem of illicit mining and smuggling, the government hurriedly introduced two stranger-specific orders/by-laws associated with The Tribal Authorities Ordinance on January 10, 1958, and published them in the Government Gazette as Public Notices. The first, the Tribal Authorities (Control of Strangers in Chiefdoms) Order, declared that the Governor permitted the Tribal Authority of chiefdoms to issue Orders "for the purpose of regulating, prohibiting and restricting the entry into or remaining within the area or any part thereof under the jurisdiction of the Tribal Authority of any stranger." The second, The Tribal Authorities (Control/Restriction of Strangers in Kono District) Order with the same provisions was specific to the seven most diamond-rich chiefdoms in Kono District—Gbense, Nimi Koro, Nimi Yema, Tankoro, Fiama, Sando, and Kamara. The orders defined a stranger as "a person who did not belong to or were not ordinarily resident in the chiefdom" (Govt. of Sierra Leone 1958b; Mitchell 2002, 238). Under this definition, Sierra Leoneans from other districts in the Sierra Leone Protectorate were now "native strangers," which conflicted with the definition in the preceding Diamond Industry Protection Ordinance. The government justified the need for the measures and painted a rosy picture of effectiveness. The annual report of the Mines Department explained:

CULTURAL DIFFERENCE

To reduce the large numbers of strangers i.e. non-Konos residing in chiefdoms in the vicinity of the Sierra Leone Selection Trust's area, the Tribal Authorities of the chiefdoms concerned subsequently made it obligatory by by-laws, for every non-native (subject to certain exceptions) of the Chiefdom to have in possession a valid Residential Permit. These measures effectively reduced the number of strangers in the area, so that towards the end of this year, conditions were much improved in the mining towns of Kono. (Govt. of Sierra Leone 1959, 4)

The government offered the incentive of stipends to chiefs to encourage them to support and implement the orders using a residential permitting system. The chiefs issued stranger residential permits to "natives" from other parts of the protectorate and "native foreigners" from other parts of West Africa. On the other hand, the District Commissioner's office handled permits for non-natives who fell into an elite group of strangers (e.g., Europeans and wealthy Lebanese and Syrians). Under the dual governance system of indirect rule in Sierra Leone as a British colony, orders as by-laws ostensibly made by Tribal Authority and enforceable in native courts were subordinate to provisions in state-level ordinances.

Some Paramount Chiefs did not approve of such regulatory measures recognizing the erosion of their traditional leadership role in governing land resources and strangers and the inherent disregard for customary etiquette to strangers (Govt. of Sierra Leone 1958b). Underpinning their concerns was the notion of illicit mining and exclusion. Host landlord-indigene communities consider themselves the rightful owners of the land and the resources on and under the ground. The chiefs are custodians on their behalf. But in the minds of the British colonial government officials, chiefs were primarily concerned because driving out strangers would affect their access to customary tribute and other remuneration (Mitchell 2002). In 1957, Paramount Chief Tamba Songu-Mbriwa of Fiama Chiefdom presented a petition on behalf of 14 Kono chiefs to the Colonial Office in London. They requested an inquiry into deteriorating social and economic conditions in the district due to diamond mining (The London Times 1957, see Figure 3.1).

Implementation of the Control of Strangers Orders was very poor. The truth was that Sierra Leoneans in both the Protectorate and the Colony were generally unhappy with colonial mining ordinances and orders/by-laws. This led to several heated debates in the governing Legislative Council. Members of the Legislative Council comprised British colonial officials and Sierra Leonean politicians, renowned citizens and Paramount Chiefs

CALL FOR SIERRA LEONE INQUIRY

THE TIMES (LONDON) 2/11/57

PETITION BY CHIEFS

A petition calling for a Royal Commission to inquire into social, economic, political, and educational conditions in Sierra Leone, with special reference to the diamond mining industry, is to be presented at the Colonial Office in London on Monday.

The petition, which bears the thumbprints of 14 paramount chiefs and tribal leaders in the Kono district, urges in particular an investigation into the recent disturbances in the district's diamond area and into allegations concerning the election of members of the Legislature.

At a Press conference in London yesterday, Dr. Edward Blyden, president of the Independent Movement of Sierra Leone, said that there had been six inquiries in Sierra Leone in the past few years. So many individual irregularities had been brought to light that now an all-embracing inquiry was needed to cover the whole question of conditions in the country. Dr. Blyden, with Mr. Tamba Mbriwra, representative for Kono in the Sierra Leone Legislature, will hand in the petition.

Mr. Mbriwra said: "It is the Sierra Leone Selection Trust that is the Government in Kono because they are in control of almost everything." P.6, Col.3

Figure 3.1 Petition by Kono chiefs to Great Britain Colonial Office, 1957.

CULTURAL DIFFERENCE 47

(customary landlords). There were 12 Districts at the time and each had an official representative or Honorable Member in the Council. Sierra Leonean members could participate in debates on policy and legislation but were unofficial members with no voting rights. They could table motions, discuss, debate, and vote on issues that they frequently did, but the Governor could overrule (Blyden 1959).

The Legislative Council debate on the Control of Strangers Orders that occurred on September 1, 1958, particularly illustrated the difficulty of integrating the African cultural notion of the stranger into mineral development policy and law. The debate revealed the reality on the ground in mining areas concerning control of strangers, categories of strangers, cultural norms, disagreements between Kono leaders on managing strangers, and power dynamics between the state and the traditional authority. Some Sierra Leoneans on the Legislative Council put forward a motion to reject the Control of Strangers in Chiefdoms Order and the Control/Restriction of Strangers in Kono District Order. A member of the Council pointed out that the redefinition of the stranger by these new orders contradicted the definition in the enabling Tribal Authorities Ordinance and was a legal violation (Govt. of Sierra Leone 1958b, 227). The Honorable Member for Kono District Council, however, argued in favor of the two orders, claiming that Kono Tribal Authorities and landlord-indigenes frustrated over uncontrollable and disrespectful strangers also supported them. Maraka diamond dealers from neighboring Guinea, in particular, were identified as ostentatious showing off their wealth from the diamond industry and causing inflation in the local economy.

Paramount Chief Mbriwa, who was chairman of the Kono District Council and cofounder of the Sierra Leone Progressive Independence Movement (SLPIM) felt that the orders "were actually thrust on the Paramount Chiefs and Tribal Authorities of Kono District" by the government and company using coercive measures (Govt. of Sierra Leone 1958b, 229). The redefinition of a stranger in the orders and the need for permits contradicted traditional norms of hospitality and etiquette to strangers. Other Sierra Leonean members of the Legislative Council who were not from the Kono District concurred with these concerns. This group articulated that the new definitions of strangers under the orders were exclusionary. They discriminated against Sierra Leoneans of other ethnicities while favoring residency in Kono of Caucasian foreigners and British subjects from the Colony (Govt. of Sierra Leone 1958b).

The motion to reject the orders passed overwhelmingly. There was a plea by a council member to amend rather than outrightly reject the motion. He suggested the removal of discriminatory clauses against Sierra Leoneans

48 CULTURE AND CONFLICTS IN SIERRA LEONE MINING

from other ethnic groups from the motion, greater empowerment of Kono chiefs to control the inflow of strangers into chiefdoms. The stranger problem was deeply undermining Kono social systems as well as SLST mining operations. The government by law had the responsibility of ensuring that the company could mine effectively. It was important for the government to support the SLST's endeavors as this would enhance the country's prestige internationally and "be an incentive to encourage further investment for our economic development" (Govt. of Sierra Leone 1958b, 241). Legislative Council member A. J. Massally, a well-respected lawyer, summarized that the government's intention was "to follow the precepts of the South African policy of 'apartheid' against natives of their own country while using as an instrument, the agency of the Tribal Authorities" (Govt. of Sierra Leone 1958b, 241–242). These motions about the stranger problem put forward and debated by Sierra Leonean members although winning by a large margin were vetoed and the orders prevailed.

There was another important motion tabled in the Legislative Council in 1958 that highlighted the stranger hierarchy in diamond areas. The motion called for a Commission of Inquiry to investigate and report upon stranger-related cases in the Magistrates Courts in Kono. The motion alleged that:

Some person or persons purposely and scrupulously went through the list of cases and transferred all "diamond" and "strangers" cases to the Court of the European District Commissioner acting in his capacity as Magistrate. (Govt. of Sierra Leone 1958b, 140)

The Council withdrew the motion before the debate commenced "for very strategic reasons." This action upset Kono chiefs in the Council who saw it as an attempt to further limit their traditional governance roles and privilege certain stranger groups (Govt. of Sierra Leone 1958b). Harry Mitchell, a 26-year-old Assistant District Commissioner in Kono District and the magistrate in question gave a firsthand account of the controversy around the matter in his narrative *Remote Corners: A Sierra Leone Memoir.* Unlike many other commissioners serving as magistrates throughout the Protectorate, he had a law degree. So, he was specifically sent to Kono District in 1958 to sit as a magistrate in countless cases on illicit mining and related lawlessness. It was clear to him that the implementation of the Control of Strangers Orders was very weak. Chiefs were not controlling native strangers or native foreigners effectively by issuing residential permits, arrests, and prosecutions in the native courts as the government envisaged. So, the government transferred cases involving strangers and illicit diamond mining to the state-level court of the District Commissioner.

CULTURAL DIFFERENCE

Mitchell had some conflict of interest concerns over his colonial administrative and judicial roles which he made known to his superior, the Provisional Commissioner of Southeastern Sierra Leone, Hugh Beattie. He described his responsibility as administering "draconian legislation," The Alluvial Mining Ordinance where "we were obliged to impose a minimum sentence of one year's imprisonment for the offense" of illicit mining (Mitchell 2002, 4, 230). Mitchell intended to be independent as a magistrate and did not unequivocally condone the official policy of mass arrests, conviction, and sentencing of strangers which was unsustainable. Even Governor Maurice Dorman, in a 1956 telegram to the Secretary of State for the Colonies, had shared his reservations about the effectiveness of the system in place to address the problem. There was a lack of infrastructure and financial resources to support a court system for mass arrests and prosecutions (TNA 554/799, 1956). Mitchell corroborated this by describing his frustration over a lack of paper to handwrite court proceedings. He proved true to his word, dismissing 100 concurrent cases based on the contradictory definitions of a stranger in the Diamond Industry Protection Ordinance and the Control of Strangers in the Kono District Order. Mitchell argued that state-level ordinances took precedence over Tribal Authority orders/by-laws.

Notwithstanding Legislative Council debates protesting the colonial government's disrespect for cultural norms and legal judgments in magistrate court, Governor Maurice Dorman went on another special tour to Kono and Kenema Districts in 1959. There, he explained the new anti-stranger orders, warned potential violators, and banned illicit mining within the SLST lease (Govt. of Sierra Leone 1961). At the time of his visit, there were an estimated 15,000 strangers in Kono District. Nevertheless, the mines department report for the year of his visit declared "there were no outbreaks of illicit mining even on a moderate scale" (Govt. of Sierra Leone 1960a, 9). The truth was that illicit mining was ongoing. The stranger problem persisted following Sierra Leone's Independence from Great Britain in 1961. In fact, by 1963, the SLST's diamond protection force comprised a well-equipped unit of 753 officers and other ranks and was still working with additional reinforcements from the Sierra Leone government's police force (Govt. of Sierra Leone 1965).

Arrests, imprisonment, and expulsion measures continued as policy following Independence. Between 1965 and 1969, 12,600 individuals were prosecuted for mining illicitly and 169 for illegal possession of diamonds. In 1968 and 1969, the protection force was considerably increased to deal with what was described as "an unprecedented wave of illicit mining" (Govt. of Sierra Leone 1970, 9). The SLST security forces in collaboration

50 CULTURE AND CONFLICTS IN SIERRA LEONE MINING

with the Sierra Leone police force carried out Operation Exodus I and II to evict "strangers" in 1969. Michael Harbottle, one-time Chief Security Officer of the SLST, conceded to the strength and organization of the illicit miners. In a memoir, *The Knave of Diamonds*, he described an unsuccessful raid at a mine site that caused serious injuries and the death of patrol officers. He concluded that the company would need strong police and helicopter support going forward. Harbottle pessimistically opined that "The day that the last diamond is mined out of its alluvial soil could be the day of salvation for Sierra Leone and its people" (Harbottle 1976, 155).

Meanwhile, the same approaches to solving the problem of illegal activity continue in postcolonial Sierra Leone. In 1971, there were 26,302 arrests and 6,090 prosecutions. "Operation Clean Slate" resulted in the expulsion of 15,000 illegal diamond diggers or *san–san boys* in 1994. Illegal activity by foreigners in the diamond industry remains a challenge (African Business 2019; Govt. of Sierra Leone 1972; Lahai Samboma 2019; Margao 2021; Marrah 2022; Reno 1995).

Postcolonial politicians continue the policy of driving away strangers from mining areas. For example, President Siaka Stevens evoked the colonial language of strangers as lawless illegal aliens at a gathering in Kono District in 1982. He told the audience that his government would not condone "the unbridled freedom that would allow strangers to plunder the country's mining fields and to smuggle produce and mineral wealth out of the country" (FBIS 1982). He did, however, give preferential treatment to some Lebanese strangers who were license holders and diamond dealers (Peters 2011). Fula elites as privileged strangers also played a dominant entrepreneurial role in the sector during his regime and that of Joseph Momoh that followed (Jalloh 2018).

President Ahmed Tejan-Kabbah in 1998 similarly addressed the stranger issue as a persistent concern in mining underscoring the cultural paradoxes in land governance. Like his predecessor, he noted the dominance of foreigners in the industry since its inception at the expense of "indigenous citizens." He temporarily suspended mining licenses owned by foreigners while his government crafted a more inclusive national mining policy that would prioritize Sierra Leonean participation in the sector (Akiwumi 2014, Fofana 1998a, 1998b). Later, in 2003, he declared the stranger problem a matter of national security because illicit miners joined the RUF/SL war from 1991 to 2001 as rebels. He held Kono chiefs responsible for not effectively managing such strangers in their chiefdoms which might have deterred discontent. The President called for a reinstatement of the landlord–stranger concept as it existed in precolonial Sierra Leone but suggested that "the Chiefs may wish in this day and age to consider dropping the 'greeting kola' tradition from the custom" (Govt. of Sierra Leone 2003).

This proposal is problematic. Due to the wealth and opportunities presented by land uses like mining, "greeting kola" or the customary gifts to landlords and chiefs today are lucrative and may include shares in mining ventures. For example, of four individual alluvial gold mining rights holders in 1952, one was a Paramount Chief and the other three were Lebanese (Govt. of Sierra Leone 1954). It is noteworthy that the Protectorate Land Ordinance of 1927 acknowledged the cultural importance of the "customary presents" sanctioned by native law to allow non-natives to reside in chiefdoms. The ordinance proposed the customary present be replaced with a fixed settler fee determined by the Governor. A non-native leasing land for a commercial venture was required to pay an annual rent. Such non-natives obtained the land with the consent of the Tribal Authority in consultation with landholding families.

The provision for annual rent for commercial endeavors by non-natives carried over into postcolonial legislation. For example, the Sierra Rutile Agreement 2002 contains clauses requiring the disbursement of a portion of rent from the company as a non-native leasing land in chiefdoms to the land holding lineages and chiefs. Lease transactions today take place in the presence of the District Officer as they did with the Governor in colonial times. Therefore, historically, chiefs have been entitled to both customary presents (settler fees) and surface rent payments for lands used for commercial purposes.

Some landlord-indigenes strongly feel that companies should respect the protocol of the customary gift or "shakehand" to their Paramount Chiefs. The SRL company made it clear that it follows its Anti-Bribery and Corruption Policy which "has strict policy requirements relating to any 'shakehand' to ensure that SRL is not involved in any improper payments" (SRK Consulting 2018a, 43). From a traditional viewpoint, this gesture is a routine part of landlord–stranger etiquette. Landlord-indigenes are entitled to a portion of profits and customary gifts for granting rights to land use and trade. Mining involves both land use and trade in minerals. One of the reasons cited for Sierra Leone's 2013 suspension from membership in the EITI was that companies had made payments to chiefs that were unreported (Remoe 2013). These examples illustrate the cultural hybridity and cultural evolution challenges in mining development. What I called "the murky waters of greeting kola, transparency, and CSR" (Akiwumi 2014).

Nevertheless, benefits to traditional elites are an incentive to support and privilege certain strangers; although a significant issue of contention between chiefs and their landlord-indigene subjects. Privileged strangers sometimes

52 CULTURE AND CONFLICTS IN SIERRA LEONE MINING

bypass landlord–stranger etiquette and protect other strangers lower down the social ladder who may disrespect customary norms. However, many strangers do find themselves marginalized, such as illicit miners exploited for labor by supporters who pay for the mining licenses and equipment. There is ambiguity in landlord relationships with strangers and the structural position of strangers does matter in the Sierra Leone mining area context.

One might argue theoretically that the state itself is complicit in empowering strangers through mining legislation to promote development goals. Multinational companies as privileged strangers lease large tracts of mineral-rich lands for extended periods through special agreements. Extraction by its very nature violates the landlord-indigenes' rights. Today, new groups of strangers other than Lebanese, Marakas, and Fulas are operating legally and illegally in the Sierra Leone mining sector as reported in the media and official documents. Some examples include Chinese, Ghanaian, Indian, Liberian, and Turkish operatives (Embassy of PRC 2018; Fallah-Williams 2021a; Marrah 2022; Thomas 2021a, 2021b).

Cultural Resistance and Illicit Mining as Protest

Another layer of cultural complexity is that the Marakas and Fulas classified as strangers or "native foreigners" in diamond mining districts have historical enclaves in Sierra Leone dating back centuries. They are counted among the 18 ethnic groups in the country and are conversant with the landlord–stranger relationship in trade, farming, and customary organization of mining. Marakas (Jula) remain respected financiers in the artisanal mining sector throughout West Africa. As such, regardless of some ambivalence over the hegemonic position of the Marakas in Sierra Leone diamond areas, host landlord-indigenes can identify with them against cultural disruption by foreign companies and the state. Landlord-indigenes express their willingness to host strangers because labor power and teamwork are essential for successful artisanal mining outcomes. Further, illicit mining as cultural resistance is a means of staking claims to customary land rights and use (Hayward 1972; Levin and Turay 2008; Villegas, Turay, and Sarmu 2013).

Colonial authorities were aware of the importance of artisanal mining as a long-time customary livelihood governed by cultural norms. For example, the annual report for 1959 documented that groups of families or village groups mined together (Govt. of Sierra Leone 1960a, 8) as would happen with farming. The scale of illicit activity forced the colonial government to recognize that there were cultural dimensions to successful outcomes. Concerning the problem in the alluvial goldfields in the 1930s and 1940s, government officials explained that they:

decided to devise a scheme which, while giving a measure of control, made it possible for natives of the Protectorate to earn their livelihoods by mining on their own behalf in those alluvial areas which they could work without needing a large capital overlay. (Govt. of Sierra Leone 1953, 6)

The AGMS introduced by Ordinance in 1946 allowed Sierra Leoneans to mine and sell gold but only to designated government buyers. The AGMS was not only to control illicit extraction but had other economic benefits for the colonial government. A decline of quickly worked gold deposits occurred by the mid-1940s, and low technology methods employed by artisanal miners would "result in a thorough cleaning up of the goldfield" (Govt. of Sierra Leone 1948, 4). A similar measure was the introduction of the Alluvial Diamond Mining Scheme (ADMS) under the Alluvial Diamond Mining Ordinance. The schemes were somewhat of an admission that the government recognized who had rightful claims to the land and its resources. The Annual Report of the Mines Department for 1955 admitted that:

little could be done to prevent illicit mining due to its scattered nature and because practically the entire populations in the areas concerned were sympathetic with the miners [...] it soon became evident that illicit mining could not be controlled so long as it was not legally possible to permit the local people to mine and sell the diamonds occurring on their lands. (Govt. of Sierra Leone 1957, 4)

The government designated several chiefdoms in the Kono, Kenema, and Bo Districts of Sierra Leone as official Alluvial Mining Areas, as well as Diamond Protection Areas. Mining licenses were determined in collaboration with the Chief Inspector of Mines, the Tribal Authority, and the landholders. Chiefs and Tribal Authorities were not involved in granting diamond dealer and exporter licenses. These were granted by the Chief Inspector of Mines and the Governor, respectively, illustrating the dominance of the state over traditional governance. The short-lived Cooperative Contract Mining Scheme (CCMS) was another venture where the SLST allowed Sierra Leoneans to mine in selected portions of its lease. The government encouraged participants in the schemes to sell diamonds found to the Government Diamond Office. Financial support was available in grants through The American Aid Revolving Loan for diamond diggers participating in the ADMS to increase output. Chiefs sometimes asked for their chiefdoms to be added to the list of Licensed Mining Areas under the schemes for revenue generation (Govt. of Sierra Leone 1938, 1952, 1962).

54 CULTURE AND CONFLICTS IN SIERRA LEONE MINING

The Mines Department assigned 50 mine wardens to supervise the schemes initially and the numbers grew over time. The first recruits were ex-servicemen of the West African Frontier Force for Britain who fought in Burma during World War II. They were responsible for regulating and monitoring compliance by individual or group license holders. Strict penalties in the form of fines, imprisonment, and cancellation of licenses were restated in the enabling legislation. Wardens received basic training in local mining law, soil conservation, and tailings disposal (Govt. of Sierra Leone 1958a). Interestingly, the person in charge of training was my late father-in-law Akiwande Akiwumi. He worked for the colonial civil service as a mining engineer, which was uncommon at the time. Some details of his story are interesting in that they reveal the cultural complexities and power relations embedded in the hierarchy of strangers in the mining areas. He was an African or Native "stranger" of Nigerian Yoruba descent. Akiwande's father S. O. Akiwumi was a wealthy entrepreneur based in Ghana who educated his children in English boarding schools followed by university or finishing school. Akiwande attended the prestigious Camborne School of Mines in Cornwall graduating as the first African mining engineer. Despite a stellar education, he could not find employment in Ghana (Gold Coast colony). There was no place for an African mining engineer in the then British-run colonial civil service. Even though he was officially designated a British subject. He worked as a surveyor for six years eventually finding a job in the Sierra Leone colonial government in 1933. His specific job title was *African* Assistant Inspector of Mines in Sierra Leone, and he was on a lower pay scale than his white counterparts, indicative of the racial discrimination in colonialism (Doortmont 2005, 84; personal communication, Akitoye Akiwumi).

The alluvial schemes exacerbated rather than solved the problem of illicit mining. The idea that the AGMS and ADMS would lead to increased government revenue because locals could mine backfired. In the case of gold, license holders were selling minerals to buyers unauthorized by the government. The quantity in ounces recorded as sold to government-sanctioned gold buyers dropped drastically. Returns were minimal compared to the number of licenses issued following the scheme's introduction. Concern grew over the local black market in gold and the loss of revenue through official channels. The Chief Inspector of Mines at the time, F. R. H. Green contended that the only satisfactory solution to the problem was for mining rights to be given to reputable commercial interests, implying that indigenous artisanal miners did not qualify as such.

This view was contradictory because before the AGMS started, the mines department had documented that the traditional tributing system

CULTURAL DIFFERENCE

was efficient. When introduced in 1937, gold production increased significantly by about half of the total production. Further, foreign companies sometimes followed locations being exploited by miners and then acquired leases for those areas. Yemen Co. Ltd. mapped out a lease where local miners had dug out gullies on a hillside at Baomahun that followed the strike of decomposed gold vein outcrops. Through the lease, they excluded others from the site and brought in machinery to break up the ore body. There was a paradox between artisanal miners as strangers, aliens, and undesirables but invaluable for working deposits that capital-intensive companies could not easily access. Indeed, the branding of mining by Sierra Leoneans as primarily illicit and economically inefficient early on was likely in response to the competition it posed to foreign-owned operations (Govt. of Sierra Leone 1938, 1948, 1954).

The colonial government poorly understood traditional artisanal mining worldviews, such as the sociocultural importance of gold in African society. From their perspective, extraction was simply a mechanical process. Miners participating in the government AGMS used the traditional gold commodity chains—the tributer system, Jula financiers, and buyers like goldsmiths. Landlord–stranger reciprocities in extraction and trade carried over with long-established alliances working together as normal. This caused the underreporting of mineral output and reduced sales to government buyers. What the government viewed as two separate licit and illicit financial flows in mineral commodity chains was in reality, one culturally hybrid commodity chain. Two modes of mining organization juxtaposed, competing and butting heads over rights, access, and control.

The government continued with prosecutions and fines for all types of gold violations that ranged from weighing minerals with a faulty scale (violation of the Weights and Measures Ordinance) to violations of sections of the Minerals Ordinance. These included unlawful mining, putting "reckless information" on an application for mining rights, unlawful possession of gold, failure to provide monthly Mineral Returns, and submitting false returns. Interestingly, even the well-established foreign company, Maroc Ltd., was found guilty of unlawful mining and fined accordingly. All details were meticulously recorded in the annual reports of the mines department (Govt. of Sierra Leone 1946; Govt. of Sierra Leone 1948).

Illicit financial flows in the gold and diamond mining sectors remain a concern in postcolonial Sierra Leone. These are informal sector activities that challenge the formal arrangements sanctioned by the state legislation. It is estimated that over 90 percent of gold mined in Sierra Leone is smuggled out of the country (CEMMATS 2021; Hunter and Smith 2017; Njini, Cohen and Kavanagh 2020). The current Sierra Leone Artisanal Mining

Policy acknowledges that artisanal mining business structures have always been informal, especially in the case of the gold industry. The government intends to integrate these informal structures into a formalized institutional framework. The Mines and Minerals Development Act of 2021 strongly supports artisanal mining as a livelihood option for Sierra Leonean citizens. The government, nevertheless, recognizes that artisanal gold mining is embedded in cultural norms:

> Most of the traders, both licensed and unlicensed, are not organized in formal entities but rather work together with their families and close friends who may serve as buying agents. The trade routes chosen and investments made are largely determined by principles of trust and loyalty in social relationships between actors within and outside the country, as well as kinship and family ties. (Govt. of Sierra Leone 2020, 61)

The artisanal sector provides livelihoods for young people and plays an important role in enhancing ethnic diversity and unity. Locals in mining areas (landlord-indigenes) and Sierra Leoneans from other ethnic groups (strangers) who in-migrate collaborate and work well together to achieve common goals (Ojukutu-Macauley and Keili 2008). However, for the first time since the first Mineral Ordinance of 1927, the term and definition of a tributer are omitted in the Mineral Act. Perhaps, this is a step toward erasure/control of the mineral trading networks that the tributer system is a part of as the government works toward formalizing the artisanal sector.

Similarly, the supporter (financier) is a carryover from the traditional system, equivalent to the Jula in gold mining. The role was accepted as part of the business structure but only recently made official by the premier Mining Law of 2021. The NMA now issues official supporter licenses and the position is now legally recognized in "official" mineral commodity chains. The government's goal is to develop a systematic approach to financing the sector that will benefit all stakeholders (Govt. of Sierra Leone 2018a). The Integrated Diamond Mining Programme (IDMP) of the USAID established a diamond mining cooperative scheme in Sierra Leone in 2005 toward formalization. The program evolved from an earlier peacebuilding intervention called the Diamond Industry Policy and Management (DIPAM) Program. The Peace Diamond Alliance (PDA) managed the scheme on the ground. Microfinance was available to local cooperatives through a revolving loan fund financed by USAID and private investors. One of the anticipated benefits was that the scheme would empower diamond diggers including "eradicating the traditional 'exploitative' supporter system" (2). After one mining season, the investors withdrew considering the scheme an economic failure. One of the reasons contributing to failure was the poor understanding of the sociocultural and historical contexts of the supporter–digger relationship. Not all diggers are "in a state of 'debt bondage' to supporters" (5). There is dependency but also reciprocity, loyalty, and trust (Levin and Turay 2008, 2, 5).

There are other challenges in formalizing the sector such as the distribution and grade of alluvial deposits following over 90 years of mining. Also, there are only a limited number of government Engineers, Mine Wardens, and Mines Monitoring Officers to monitor and inspect mining operations and resolve disputes. Therefore, sometimes chiefdom councils and chiefdom mining committees carry out supervisory functions just as they would customarily. These are all illustrations of the cultural hybridity between the traditional and state approaches to mining organizations.

Illegal activities have always been rampant in the diamond industry since its inception. The rush to diamond areas early on was critical as it drew labor away from "legitimate" mines like the Sierra Leone Chrome Mining Company Ltd. The mine was relatively close to the diamond fields, so its operations were most adversely affected. Some miners even abandoned the AGMS in favor of a higher-value mineral. At the height of the diamond rush in the 1950s, well-organized groups of illicit miners in the thousands would invade the SLST lease at night. Security forces were inadequate to deal with the problem and often security posts were attacked and personnel wounded or killed. Miners also ambushed company vehicles. The company's Beaver Aircraft would fly overhead to spot miners and inform ground security units (Govt. of Sierra Leone 1960a, 11; Harbottle 1976).

A reluctant government increasingly acknowledged those people who had legitimate rights to the land despite colonial ordinances to the contrary. Statements in government and company reports began to address cultural heritage and its connection to antisystemic protests against the cultural disruption and cultural imperialism caused by foreign mining management. Stranger and landlord-indigene alliances worked against foreign companies perceived as the most powerful strangers. The SLST lamented that its Sierra Leonean security hires and the Sierra Leone police assigned to protecting company installations shared the traditional view of land ownership that cast doubts on their loyalty and commitment to the company as their employer (Govt. of Sierra Leone 1955, 1956).

A landlord-indigene organization called the Kono Progressive Movement (KPM) strongly criticized the whole business of strangers mining on ancestral lands. As Hayward (1972, 10–11) elaborated:

58   CULTURE AND CONFLICTS IN SIERRA LEONE MINING

The KPM was basically against the idea that the British people and other strangers could come and take things from underground in Kono. The Kono people felt it was their right to part or all of its value. Kono people regarded the diamonds on Kono lands as the rightful assets of the Kono people and not of the government, a foreign company, or other "strangers."

Because of this conviction, artisanal mining was widespread and generally acceptable by the Kono people. Mining groups were well organized and often utilized lookouts and guards. Periodic successful attacks on the security patrols of the SLST and the Sierra Leone police were reported with pride and a sense of justice. Kono benefiting, somehow from diamond wealth, was only fair considering the injustices allowed by legislation. It was a redistribution of community wealth to the rightful beneficiaries (Conteh 1979).

In a more current example of artisanal mining conflicts between foreign companies and host communities, colonial patterns in the government's response to the problems are still apparent. The Minister and Deputy Minister of Mines and Mineral Resources visited the Bombali District in 2013 to inform landlord-indigene communities that a company called AMR Gold was legally mandated by the government to prospect for coltan under an exclusive license. Another foreign company was also claiming mining rights issued by the Ministry of Mines and Mineral Resources for coltan, diamonds, gold, and zircon. The ministers warned the communities against condoning and participating in illicit mining. The activity, nevertheless, continued in Bombali District with both foreign and local actors participating. In addition, attempts by competing foreign companies to co-opt some landowners into supporting exploration activities caused tension within the communities. To demonstrate control of the problem, the government temporarily banned the mining of coltan and zircon in 2013 (AYV 2013). For the landlord-indigene communities, coltan mining is an alternative subsistence livelihood, a means to diversify income and alleviate poverty. The recent 2021 mining law addresses the issue of unfair mining negotiations and revenue sharing in artisanal mining for Sierra Leoneans. The implementation may take a while to fully realize the benefits.

The Ministry of Mines and the National Mineral Agency are primarily responsible for the campaign to arrest and persecute violators. In July 2018, authorities arrested 38 illegal Chinese miners for gold mining in Kono District. Ten of them pled guilty and received sentences of two years in prison or a $2,000 fine (Villa 2018). The Embassy of China in response posted a notice to Chinese businesses and citizens urging them to follow the mining and environmental policies and laws of Sierra Leone (Embassy of PRC

CULTURAL DIFFERENCE 59

2018). In 2021, a coalition of the Ministry of Mines, the National Mineral Agency, the Ministry of Internal Affairs, the Police, the Immigration Department, and the Office of National Security and Labor and Information carried out major raids in Kono and Tonkolili Districts on illicit "foreign miners." The nationalities arrested included Indians, Ghanaians, and some Sierra Leoneans. The government destroyed or dismantled numerous dredges and other mining machinery (Vandy 2021). It is against the law to use dredges in the designated lease size allowed for artisanal mining by Sierra Leoneans, only. Lease owners with little capital, oftentimes, partner with foreigners as investors who bring in machinery and equipment used in violations.

In the colonial period, annual reports of the mines department kept systematic and meticulous statistics and records of the mineral industry including such challenges. In the postcolonial period, government mining reports and documents are comparatively irregular due to events like the 10-year RUF/SL war and other constraints. However, the Sierra Leone Extractive Industries Transparency Initiative (SLEITI) annual reports record mining sector information under designated categories of stakeholders engagement, transparency, accountability, revenue generated, governance/ management structure, and enabling environment. Sierra Leone joined the EITI in 2006 but became a compliant country in 2014. There are 10 SLEITI reports since 2013. A detailed analysis of five of the nine reports revealed that illegal diamond mining remains a problem. A major challenge is that the activity often occurs in remote areas of the country. Monitoring by the government requires a tremendous amount of financial and manpower resources which is lacking (Margao 2021). Other sources providing information on the mining industry are research studies, company Environmental, Social and Health Impact Assessments (ESHIAs), consultancy reports, and media articles.

The word "stranger" is not explicitly used in postcolonial land and mining policies and laws. For example, the Diamond Protection Regulation of 2013 uses citizen and noncitizen designations. In the popular press and government documents, terms for strangers include illegal or illicit foreign miners, foreigners, noncitizens, or non-natives. However, the country's NLP of 2015 recognized the importance of customary land governance systems and that a landlord–stranger institution is a form of customary tenancy. The document explained that:

> In former times, this was the commonest way by which strangers in the chiefdom and persons who were not entitled as of right to access to land, acquired land for agricultural or building purposes.

60 CULTURE AND CONFLICTS IN SIERRA LEONE MINING

> The process is sometimes described by the use of the terms "begging" and "loan." A person in need of the land was expected to "beg" for it from the chief or a landowning family and the latter would "loan" the land in accordance with well-established practices and principles of customary law. (Govt. of Sierra Leone 2015c, 49)

The NLP states that the customary land tenure systems are the primary legal entities on land matters for the majority of Sierra Leoneans. The government intends to strengthen them "to facilitate and promote its orderly evolution into a modern productive land tenure system" (Govt. of Sierra Leone 2015c, 8). Indeed, the recently enacted laws, The National Land Commission Act of 2022 and The Customary Land Rights Act of 2022, are bold documents focusing on a more democratic approach to land governance and rights equity for women and non-natives (strangers) in provincial areas. The National Land Commission Act repeals the colonial Protectorate Lands Ordinance of 1927 (later the Provinces Land Act), which vested all Protectorate lands in Tribal Authorities (now Chiefdom Councils). To recap, headed by the Paramount Chief, these bodies held land for and on behalf of land holding communities and strongly influenced decisions on administration and management (Govt. of Sierra Leone 2022a).

The Customary Land Rights Act of 2022 now assigns this responsibility to Chiefdom Land Committees. The Paramount Chief or a representative will chair the committee comprising landowners, female representatives (30%), and land users (strangers), but the people of the chiefdom as a community have ownership and title of communal lands. Specifically, "members of the Chiefdom Land Committee are accountable to members of the community for any decisions made about the community's landholdings" (Govt. of Sierra Leone 2022b, 29–30). Reviews of the laws are mixed. NAMATI (The Legal Empowerment Network) described the law as unprecedented and a blueprint for the rest of the world to address environmental justice and customary land rights issues (NAMATI 2022). Advocates for women's rights see the law as a victory for women. Other opinions expressed are that conflict-free implementation of the law requires adequately addressing tradition and culture such as land ties based on ethnicity and origin (Peltier 2022). This is the foundation of the landlord–stranger institution. Invest Salone, a UK government-funded, private sector development program that partners with businesses, government, and civil society to promote responsible investment raised several concerns, also. These included length of leases, size of leases, land valuation, challenges administering the laws at the local level of chiefdoms, and "broad ambiguous wording" in the laws (INVEST SALONE 2022).

The Sierra Leone Minerals Policy 2018 pays more attention to cultural dynamics in the mining sector compared to the earlier 2003 version. Although not using the term "stranger," the document describes the continuing challenges of what is the enduring "stranger issue":

> Internal migration of workers as well as increased foreign participation has occurred in minerals development activities throughout Sierra Leone. These have had social, cultural and religious impacts on mining communities. More understanding of these issues to address how these impacts will affect the country is required. (Govt. of Sierra Leone 2018a, 45)

The document further references the grievances and social protests around mineral exploitation and the need for better community-based conflict mitigation and dispute resolution strategies. In this regard, the government acknowledges the important role of cultural norms in these processes. So, the government will promote and facilitate "localized/customized mechanisms relevant to mine affected communities that consider cultural and traditional practices" (27). Further, "harmonization with specific emphasis on Chiefdom mineral land management is deemed to be in the national interest" (49). The Mineral Policy documents that conflicts and violence due to unresolved land disputes, involuntary resettlement, and illegal mining negatively impact mineral commodity chains. Production oftentimes stops, and expensive mine equipment and infrastructure are damaged adding to the operations costs of companies and decreasing revenue for the nation (Govt. of Sierra Leone 2018a, 27, 49). This reality of cultural conflicts impacting commodity chains echoes Governor Dorman's concern at the dawn of Sierra Leone's independence from Great Britain—that the intractable illegal digging and smuggling of diamonds by strangers was the reason for the heavy budget deficit of the colony (Bigart 1960).

Mining companies also recognize that cultural matters can affect their bottom line and try to address them. An ESHIA for the Sierra Rutile Expansion report for the rutile mining area documented "the stranger issue" going a step further to suggest some management and mitigation strategies. Results of household surveys highlighted an influx of nonlocal people seeking potential job or business opportunities causing community disruption. Boom towns like Moriba Town and Mogbwemo, according to locals, are mostly where "outsiders and imported labour from other parts of Sierra Leone" live. The ESHIA recommended that to manage and mitigate the in-migration, SRL, local leadership, and external stakeholders should develop and implement an Influx Management Plan (SRK 2018a, 32).

Another cultural conflict issue of concern to companies and communities is the interconnectedness between land, livelihoods, and spirituality and the importance of sacred places. As mentioned earlier, these sacrosanct spaces such as sacred or society bushes are important to land management, community cohesion, and cultural sustainability. Mining oftentimes destroys them. In Chapter 4, I discuss sacred places and conflicts in Sierra Leones mining areas and how the government addresses the matter in policies and laws and companies' responses.

Chapter 4

SACRED PLACES: LOCAL ONTOLOGY MEETS GLOBAL CAPITAL

[...] superstitions were constantly interfering with my plans, but most maddening of all to a geologist was the sacred bush around the villages, into which no white person was permitted to go under any circumstances, for it is the haunt of those initiated into the secret societies. Iron and gold might lie all over the ground, but I couldn't even set my foot into this territory. (Fowler-Lunn 1938, 101)

Writings of the late Sierra Leonean scholar of African theology, Harry Sawyerr, *God: Ancestor or Creator?* (1970) and *The Practice of Presence* (1968) discuss God in traditional West African religion. He is the supreme being, creator, omnipotent, the Great Ancestor, and "a living God who can do for human beings what nobody else can" (Sawyerr 1970, 4). In Sierra Leone, the Mende calls him *Ngewo*, the Kono, *Yataa* and the Temne, *Kurumasaba*. Ancestral spirits are intermediaries between God and humans as ancestors remain an integral part of the family, clan, and ethnic group. There is an intricate relationship between spirituality and nature. Ceremonies involving the ancestors occur at sacred places such as forests, bushes, trees, water bodies, caves, stones, and shrines generally categorized as the sacred bush. In the traditional worldview, it is sacrilegious to violate revered places, and trees in the sacred bush should not be cut down. In precolonial times, that sacrilege was punishable by death. Today, arbitrators might levy heavy fines on the guilty (Fenton 1948). A major area of conflict between communities and mining companies is the desecration and/or destruction of such places. Many sites of religious significance to landlord-indigene communities in Sierra Leone have been lost to mining. This loss continues as extraction expands in the country. I document some examples of lost sites that are also of anthropological interest. I also discuss how government policies and laws address the sacred bush and other cultural heritage matters.

Christian missionaries observed strong religious beliefs, spirituality, and attachments to sacred places of worship among Sierra Leoneans. These proselytizers and others did not fully understand the underpinning worldview such as the important role of ancestors and responsibilities to future generations. Rituals at sacred sites were viewed as primitive, superstition, or witchcraft that ideally should be eradicated. District Commissioner Thomas Alldridge was intrigued by a sacred, crystal clear pool inhabited by the so-called fetish fish at Kenema Town shown in Figure 4.1. He described in some detail the beauty and serenity of the place and his observation of a recitation by an elder at the water body. Alldridge assumed that the local people worshipped the fish because they fed them, protected their habitat, and did not eat them. He concluded that "there is no doubt the people of Kennema have a very implicit belief in the occult powers of their 'fetish fish'" (Alldridge 1910, 156). The popular Creole photographer Lisk-Carew who took the picture similarly reflected the ignorance and prejudice of the time labeling the image "fetish fish pond."

A missionary of the Evangelical United Brethren, Reverend Parker E. Young, wrote a short piece titled "Diamond Mines Offer a Great Challenge" in *The Evangel*, the bulletin of the Evangelical United Brethren Church. Based in Kono District in 1937, he saw diamond mining as a great opportunity to recruit Christian converts, migrant miners alienated from their traditional religious beliefs in unfamiliar territory. Young wrote of the miner's "separation

Figure 4.1 Fetish fish pond, Kenema Town circa 1910.

SACRED PLACES

from the place where his ancestral spirits reside." He posed the rhetorical question: What are we doing to meet this need—the need of a man caught in a changing culture? More importantly, he acknowledged a "changing culture which is being forced upon the African" (Young 1937, 11–12). Forces such as translocal religionists, modernization, and Western urbanization continue to erode the sustainability of traditional sacred institutions that govern life and livelihoods (Boone 1986; Fanthorpe 2007).

In traditional beliefs, minerals occur on land and in waters that are also the home of spirits. Hills, water bodies like lakes and rivers, and caves are important sacred places where communities hold annual ceremonies and rites. To carry out artisanal mining and mineral processing as successful livelihoods, miners must establish a good relationship with the spirits. To do so, miners carry out appropriate rituals to communicate with them (D'Angelo 2014; Ferme 2000). Inland freshwater lakes such as Sonfon, Mabesi, and Mape are places of historic, cultural, and religious significance. Lake Sonfon (or Lake Confon) in the Sula Mountains is the largest and is the source of the Pampana River. Situated in Diang Chiefdom, Koinadugu District, it is a sacred place to the Koranko ethnic group who settled in the vicinity in the sixteenth to seventeenth centuries led by Mansa Beaty. Warrior strangers joined them and they agreed to coexist. The Koranko as landlords with spiritual attachment to the lake carried out land management and the warriors, political governance. The most powerful djinn or spirit of the lake is Yeremu Dala (Queen of a Huge Castle in the Koranko language) who inhabits a part of the lake called Dala Feh. The landlord-indigenes hold ceremonies and rituals at the lake to propitiate her and other revered spirits that guard, guide, and protect the communities. These early inhabitants coexisted with the diverse wildlife in the area. An influx of mine workers since the late 1920s has caused a decline in animal species hunted for food and extraction has destroyed their habitats (Jackson 2011; Sesay 2023).

Reverend W. T. Harris of the Methodist Mission in colonial Sierra Leone documented some other sacrosanct places like Kwi Kongo and Leopard Hill in Kono District. In the old days, the forested hill was home to wildlife including bush cows, leopards, porcupines, and rock rabbits. Some white birds living there were protected as hallowed property of the spirit. It was also a conservation area and burning and clearing to farm was forbidden. An annual sacrifice led by a prayer leader was made to the Spirit of the Hill. A water spirit also lived in a stream flowing through the hill. The hill fell within the SLST lease and became part of the Reservation with bungalows for Caucasian expatriate employees. Harris wrote how before the lease "all the adult males in that part of the Kono country met on the slope of the hill behind what is now the

66 CULTURE AND CONFLICTS IN SIERRA LEONE MINING

Number 10 bungalow." The ceremony at this famous location ended in the 1930s when the company acquired the lease (Harris 1954, 96).

Harris described another religious event on the banks of the Moa River associated with a community hunting expedition that included sacrifices and libations to the ancestor spirits living in the river depths and feasting. The prayer leader or *Humoi* recited:

> You in the water, this is yours [...] Help us in our farm work, let the rain come to make our rice good, let the danger from the water miss us, take care of our children, let them not walk on the hot earth. Take care of the big men and save our women.

A prayer response *Ngewo Jahu* followed, which means: "by God's power may it be so" (Harris 1954, 94–95).

When diamonds were found in Kenema, Bo, Bonthe, and Pujehun Districts in the lower reaches of the Moa and Sewa Rivers in 1935, the colonial government protected the interests of the company, The Order in Council, Rivers Sewa and Moa Closed Areas to Prospecting Order (No. 24 of 12 December 1935), declared diamond-rich lands along the river as a closed area (van der Laan 1965, 44). This limited access to some sacred places as well as artisanal mining by communities along the river.

Parts of the River Moa remain the site of community ceremonies even today. The river, for instance, was at the center of the symbolic reparation held in eastern Sierra Leone as part of the postwar Truth and Reconciliation Commission (TRC) National Reparation Programme. The ceremony entailed a symbolic reburial of all the residents of the chiefdom killed during the RUF/SL rebel war and denied a proper funeral. The deliberations involved purification by participants and symbolic cleansing of the River Moa of the sins of the war years (Awareness Times 2009).

Sylvia Ardyn Boone (1986) in her comprehensive work on Sande, *Radiance from the Waters: Ideals of Feminine Beauty in Mende Art* documented that the *Sande* organization manages the affairs of traditional women teaching initiates valuable life skills like agricultural techniques, fine arts, herbal medicine, morality, and leadership. Scoop-net fishing by wading into rivers, swamps, or creeks is the realm of women, a notion respected by males. Rivers are sacred with water as "mystical space, the medium of love and life before life (107). During rites of passage, initiates or *Mbogboni* (meaning water people) congregate in the *Kpanguima*, sited near water like "the river depths where spirits enjoy a divine existence of beauty and peace" (50). Religious artifacts and paraphernalia, such as Sowo masks, are buried under water. Items are retrieved by a diver who is senior in the organization's hierarchy for special ceremonies.

Symbols on masks teach moral and philosophical life lessons to initiates worthy of sharing. These include intelligence (Nemahulewe [nemahulengo]), stamina (Kahu [kahungo]), responsibility (Kpaya [kpayango]), persistence (Di [dingo], endurance of hardship (Malondo [malondongo]), truthfulness (Tonya [tonyango]), straightforwardness/reliability (Pona [ponango]), and courage (Ndilo [Ndilongo]) literally translated as "the heart can bear up." Boone asked the Sande elders why there was no symbol for "generosity." The response was that it was innately understood that: "One can never be too generous. All that is possible to do for others should be done" (Boone 1986, 37). Mining activities have desecrated many long-established sites central to passing on such values. Figure 4.2 illustrates an impasse with a mining bulldozer at the sacred bush at Tefeya village, Kono District, in 2006.

Figure 4.2 Sacred bush at Tefeya Village, Kono District, 2006.

68   CULTURE AND CONFLICTS IN SIERRA LEONE MINING

Village relocation to facilitate mining is the primary cause of this as sacred sites are close to or inside settlements. I witnessed this firsthand in the titanium mineral dredging operations areas in Moyamba and Bonthe Districts. Dammed rivers create reservoirs or dredge ponds that flood villages and farmlands. Mining commenced in 1963 and by 2001, there were 14 relocated villages. The company might think that financial compensation for village relocations is enough but the cultural and religious ramifications for inhabitants are far greater. For example, Sierra Rutile moved 200-year-old Imperi (Mbellah) over six months. This village had great historic significance and was a famous divination center. A sacred site, *Solondo* or "Foot in the Stone," inhabitants say bears the footprints of the revered founding warriors of the village. The inhabitants were relocated from their ancestral lands and burial places to mine the Lanti rutile deposit. I vividly remember a trip to the Lanti catchment in 1991, where the richest and most extensive rutile deposit lies during the land clearing phase. The topography here changes dramatically from the Gbangbama and Imperi Hills to the north and east of the catchment, respectively, to gently undulating plains 15 meters a.s.l. extending southwesterly toward the coast. In the vicinity of the already constructed dam C3, we drove past the remains of Imperi village. My colleague driving the vehicle instinctively turned in along the dirt road leading to the deserted site. A half-finished canoe carved out of a tree trunk, a broken clay pot next to three firestones, and a head of bananas on a wilting tree – all lay abandoned. No one spoke a word, as if we had agreed upon a moment of silence in respect for the soul of the dead village.

Mining operations also affected deleteriously the Elephant Well, a sacred spring and water hole used in ritual purification at Old Vaama. This was a natural spring that village folklore says was dug by elephants who used it as a watering hole (Akiwumi 1987). Elephants were plentiful in the area in the past and missionary George E. Thompson described an encounter with a family in the nineteenth century (Thompson 1969). The spring was in the middle of an enclave of trees with a clearing. Very strict laws were applied to its use and protection. No one could enter the area with dirty feet or use just any container to draw the water. The aura surrounding its origin and its use provided some pollution control. It was lost when the village moved.

Another example was a church at Pejebu built in 1987 that had striking murals of Biblical scenes depicting African saints and angels painted by local artists. It was demolished shortly after completion when the company relocated the village to construct a dam. The inhabitants of this region have a long association with Christianity dating back to the mid-nineteenth century through the American Missionary Association and the Evangelical United Brethren (United Methodist Church). The relocation of Pejebu was a moral dilemma for the company's general manager who was moved by the beautiful church and had considered postponement. The destruction of and separation from this holy place was traumatic for the local people. It was demolished and buried in a noisy grave; no R.I.P. with the 24-hour grinding of the dredges in Pejebu pond until the ore was exhausted. Semabu village situated close to mangroves with its picturesque forms of traditional architecture also moved. Several years after leaving Sierra Leone, the manager shared with me that Old Semabu was his favorite village and he "really felt he could relate to the village people who were understandably reluctant to move" (personal communication, April 10, 1993).

New and more modern relocation villages do not always compensate for the loss of old sites. Villagers sometimes boycott newly constructed facilities, such as community centers, at relocation sites in protest over involuntary resettlement. The Organization for Research and Extension of Intermediate Technology (OREINT), a local NGO, collaborated with Friends of the Earth, UK, in the 1990s to gather survey information that revealed animosity toward the company and bitterness over the loss of sacred sites. Local people vigorously expressed concerns and anxiety about the possible relocation of the villages of Hemabu, Jangaloh, and Nyandehun in the mine lease. These villages are historic centers of herbal medicine and divination dating back to precolonial times (Alie 2001; Kamara 1997; Knight Piesold 2001). Figure 4.3 shows a ceremony at a sacred site in the rutile lease taken in the 1980s.

Figure 4.3 Sacred place in rutile lease, 1980s.

Sacred bush conflicts continue and are over loss or desecration, compulsory acquisition, valuation, and compensation. The mining industry since colonial times recognized and responded to conflicts over sacred places. The Minerals Ordinance of 1927 prohibited mining from on, under, or 100 yards away from land habitually used or occupied for sacred or ceremonial purposes, or burial grounds without written permission of the Governor. Foreign geologists expressed frustration over the enforcement of the clause as it impacted fieldwork evidenced by Katharine Fowler-Lunn, an American quoted above. Another geologist with the rutile mining company in 1972, likewise, showed poor cultural understanding and sensitivity to sacred bush around the villages of Imperi and Nyandehun. He wrote from a company perspective that two areas of sacred bush were likely encroaching on the ore deposit "so locals were using the space at their own risk" (Claus, Padgett et al. 1972, 69).

The position on sacred places has evolved in subsequent versions of the premier Mineral Law. The current 2021 Mines and Minerals Development requires the consent of an authorized agent for mining "land dedicated as a place of burial, or of religious or other cultural significance." It also omits the reference to permission to enter the "sacred bush" as mentioned in the 1994 and 2009 versions. An application for a dredging permit should report if the process will destroy sacred places, burial grounds, or monuments and relics. Under the "general obligations to promote community development," companies are "to safeguard customs, tradition and religion that can reasonably be expected to development/to be impacted by license activities." This is a modification of the more emphatic clause in the 1994 and 2009 versions where companies "shall recognize and respect the rights, customs, traditions and religion of local communities."

Reference to sacred places and cultural heritage matters vary in special agreements for bauxite, diamonds, iron ore, and rutile extraction. Typical clauses in these agreements alluding to cultural sensitivity are "The company shall respect and cause its employees and contractors to respect the customs of the local populations" or the company "shall at all times do everything reasonable in its power to limit the damage and disturbance to the local environment and populace." The London Mining Agreement 2012 adopted the clause from the Mining Law of 2009. The company must have written permission to enter "any land dedicated as a place of burial or which is a place of religious or other cultural significance." The more ambiguous nature of recent modifications provides a loophole for interpretation by companies that could lead to conflicts. None of these agreements make specific mention of the sacred bush.

However, companies do document them in impact assessment reports and typically have ad hoc policies to address sacred bush, cultural heritage,

SACRED PLACES 71

and the inevitable related conflicts. I discuss some examples below (Govt. of Sierra Leone, various years; National Minerals Agency 2023). Mining companies experience on the ground that sacred places are a major conflict issue. The ESHIA done for AML in 2010 documented the cultural importance of sacred bushes or forests. The report recognized that villages throughout rural Sierra Leone have sites nearby as they are places of spiritual significance and provide useful forest resources. In the landscape mosaic created by shifting cultivation and mining activities, sacred forests/bushes are mostly the only remnants of primary vegetation (WorleyParsons Ltd. 2010). A 1996 ethnographic survey for a feasibility study for the Bumbuna Hydroelectric Project that overlaps with the AML lease revealed details of sacred sites in 20 Kalantuba Limba villages. The *Gbangbani* sacred grove or *bembe* is where "the people assemble before embarking on any significant function or undertaking." They documented water features including the Bumbuna waterfalls and streams closest to settlements ("the holy water place" or *kamatane*) as sacrosanct. Although there were variations in ritual ceremonies between villages, the sacred grove at the historic village of Kadala (now relocated) was revered as the oldest, where joint intervillage ceremonial activities took place (Abraham and Gaima 1996, 20).

Foa Matturie, a Kono chief, was one of the first landlords to protest the desecration of sacred institutions from diamond mining in 1934 and demand compensation. His protest led eventually to the introduction of a compensation scheme for sacred bush sites. Sorie J. Conteh discussed the cultural conflict inherent in negotiations in his 1979 work on *Diamond Mining and Kono Religious Institutions*. The company agreed to pay the costs to cover reconsecration at new sacred bush sites. The District Commissioner (DC) for Kono District as national government mediator stipulated a rate of compensation in a written, but not legal, agreement between the chief and Tribal Authorities, the SLST company, and the national government in 1966. It was a bona fide effort by the company, which provided a surveyor to demarcate an area chosen by local people. There was a back-and-forth exchange between parties with ad hoc policy evolving in negotiations through letters between company and chiefdom leaders. A Sacred Bush Demarcation and Compensation Memorandum I of May 1967 listed detailed rules and guidelines for the basis of compensation. This led to the classification, demarcation, and registration of numerous sacred bush sites in 1967 and 1968.

Some controversy ensued over adequate compensation and renegotiating claims. A letter from SLST's Acting General Manager dated September 20, 1969 to the District Commissioner accused the Tribal Authorities of using sacred places for monetary gain. Accusations included creating fictitious sacred bush sites for illegal mining and submitting false compensation claims.

72 CULTURE AND CONFLICTS IN SIERRA LEONE MINING

Indignant Kono retorted that they had never sold their land to the company and that they had the right to exploit resources on their ancestral lands.

Notwithstanding claims of illegal mining activity, Conteh revealed the trauma of cultural disruption and cultural alienation from the loss of historic sacred sites. Lake Moindema on the Moinde River in Kamara Chiefdom was a sacrosanct place for the Kono but a diamond-rich location from the company's perspective. This place was a haven for centuries for Kono people fleeing the many intertribal wars that were common in the historic past. Ceremonies paying homage to the ancestors there was an important part of cultural heritage and cultural sustainability, and the lake was fished twice a year. When the company decided to mine the rich alluvial diamond deposits in the lake, they and the chiefdom people could not agree on the requested compensation amount. The company felt that the amount was exorbitant and argued that the Kono sacrificing the mineral-rich lake would provide revenue to benefit the whole country. SLST began constructing a canal and mining while negotiations were in progress and before the Kono could remove sacred items from the lake. In anger, the affected people physically blocked access to the mining site. The Chiefdom Authorities wrote a strong protest letter to the Prime Minister on June 18, 1969 asking:

> What foreigner would have the temerity to invade their lodges and esoteric places in Europe? None. Well, then, why do it to us? We strongly protest against the pollution of our sacred bush and we shall submit our case to a Court of Justice. (Conteh 1979, 190)

Complaints about violations of sacred places continue. A multistakeholder consultative workshop on land reclamation and alternative land use was held in Koidu, the main town in diamond mining Kono District, February 8–9, 2007, sponsored by USAID and the Foundation for Environmental Security and Sustainability (FESS). Participants were asked to identify the challenges of land reclamation in alluvial diamond mining communities. Concerns raised included the impact of strangers on Kono cultural values and practices and the loss of traditional landmarks, boundaries, and sacred bush (forest). Reclamation should involve restoring poro bush sites (FESS 2007).

Recent sacred place conflicts occurred at the African Minerals iron ore mine in Tonkolili District in 2010 and 2012. On both occasions, the government police responded each time with tear gas and the beating of protestors. In 2010, The African Minerals company determined that the optimum location to construct a dam was outside the lease in an area that was a water supply source, farmland, and a village sacred bush of

SACRED PLACES

Kemedugu village. The local people in protest held two African Minerals hostage and later released them (Akam 2010; McClanahan 2010).

The 2012 strike was on a larger scale and took place in the town of Bumbuna. Landlord-indigenes and stranger coalitions set up roadblocks so that company vehicles could not reach the mine site. The government sent in police to contain the strike and the company provided logistical support (vehicles, money, and accommodation) to the police. A group of 50 women, comprising company workers and local community residents, resorted to Bondo/Sande's customary modes of protest. Carrying green twigs, they marched peacefully through the town. Police sent in by the government to contain the strike opened fire on them and a woman employed by an African Minerals contractor was killed (Human Rights Watch 2014).

This action by police as state representatives showed disregard for a historic cultural organization that plays an important and central role in women's lives in rural Sierra Leone (Boone 1986; Ibrahim-Fofana et al. 2019; Phillips 1995). Disrespecting the organization and its values is problematic for cultural sustainability. Indeed Boone (1986, xvii) explained that the Sande elders she interviewed were mindful of the potential for cultural disruption and cultural alienation triggered by "the tides of westernization and Islamization that are bringing great changes to traditional life."

To compound the situation, some locals injured in the attack by police took AML to court in England (Kadie Kalma & Ors. v. African Minerals Ltd And Ors [2020] EWCA Civ 144). Both the English Court and the Court of Appeal dismissed the claims in favor of the company. The judgment was that "whilst companies operating abroad may properly help to facilitate the law and order expected to be provided by host countries, it is the governments of those countries (and not the companies) who have the primary responsibility to promote and protect human rights" (Hughes Jennett and Hood 2020).

Monetary compensation continues as an ad hoc policy but is still not considered enough by communities. In 2010, AML's Social and Community Relations Manager acknowledged that work for a proposed dam site destroyed sacred bush, commercial trees, and fertile farmland. It offered a monetary compensation package to affected farmers in the chiefdoms of Kafe, Kalasogoia, and Sambaya Bendugu. African Minerals for the destruction of the sacred bush were considered inadequate (Kabba 2010).

The SRL has compensated for sacred bushes, burial grounds, shrines, churches, and mosques. For example, the "SRL Resettlement Action Planned Compensation and Entitlement Framework" for Foinda village listed the Bondo house, secret society bush site, and graves as items for compensation. The area town planning officer would assess the cost of replacing the Bondo house structure for cash compensation. The cash

74   CULTURE AND CONFLICTS IN SIERRA LEONE MINING

compensation to reconsecrate the new sacred bush would be agreed upon with the community. Other sacred places like the church and mosque at the new village site would be rehabilitated. The cash compensation for graves at the new village site would be agreed upon by stakeholders including the Sierra Leone government (Knight Piesold 2001). However, a 2018 social impact assessment by SRL quoted the sentiments of a community resident about the state of sacred places for social and religious ceremonies—ancestral cemeteries, the Poro and Bondo society bushes, shrine bushes, and caves, today:

> The mining activities of SRL have completely cleared all these bushes and none is left as a monument for the future generations. The cultural heritage of the local people is no more. The customs and traditions of the local communities are flouted with impunity [...] What a pity. (SRK Consulting 2018b, 44)

This responsibility of present-day communities to future generations is a matter of great concern. Similarly, the town chief of Worowaia village and a member of the NGO Save Lake Sonfon both expressed disappointment that there would be no history or cultural heritage to share with unborn generations due to the mining transformation of the landscape. This reality violates the underpinnings of sustainable development as envisaged from mineral exploitation (Schwartz 2006). The idea that mining companies disregard sacred places and cultural practices is also addressed in the popular media. Newspaper articles periodically report public opinion on the importance of honoring rituals to appease the ancestral spirits of lands and waters violated by mining to ensure success with mineral extraction and community and mine workers' safety. A writer in *The Eagle* newspaper in 1992 opined that a combination of customary rituals to appease spirits inhabiting mineral-rich lands and good government mining policy might control illegal mining and smuggling by strangers and aliens. Foreigners, the writer wrote, benefit from "the golden opportunities of mining diamonds in Kono" at the expense of Sierra Leoneans who host strangers to their disadvantage (The Eagle 1992, 4).

Mining companies sometimes comply with honoring local customs by covering the costs of ritual items and other expenses for ceremonies. In 1984, the local Paramount Chief at Marampa organized an appeasement ritual at the Austro Minerals iron ore mine. The company funded the event seeing it as an opportunity to span "cultural and hierarchical divides between mine and communities." Labeled the "devil ceremony," it included the sacrifice of cows, which disgusted and amazed Austrian mineworkers who had never seen

SACRED PLACES

anything like it (Hauser 2013, 70). In 2010, the London Mining Company (LMC) operating at the Marampa mine, likewise, showed sensitivity to cultural heritage matters. It provided financial assistance as part of its corporate social responsibility (CSR) to the landlord host community to observe an important cultural tradition, the Kantha Ritual Rites of Paramount Chief Bai Koblo Queen II (Awoko Publications, 2010).

In another example, disregard for such rituals was considered the cause of a major accident at the SRL mine in June 2008. A newly constructed dredge named for the famous historic warrior *Solondo* capsized with 50 people aboard, and two workers drowned. The death on the same day of Sierra Rutile's Chief Geologist from a heart attack while on vacation in Australia compounded the explanation. In reaction to the dredge accident, considerable anger and grief consumed the communities in Imperi Chiefdom, Bonthe District, where the accident occurred. Adding to the trauma was the fact that the bodies of the two drowned workers could not be found for customary burial rites. The incident uncovered festering grievances about the company's disregard for customary worldview and the cultural and environmental costs of mining to communities. Following the accident, the company responded to the request by the Paramount Chief and chiefdom elders for a ceremony to appease ancestral spirits and financed items needed (D'Angelo 2019; Massaquoi and Hill 2008; Sesay 2008; Standard Times 2008).

The dredge did have technical flaws, a problem that had occurred with a dredge at this mine in the past. The report of the government mines division for 1965–1969 documented that the rutile company "met with a considerable amount of technical difficulties and calamities, one such being the capsizing of the dredge on 27 December 1967." Problems with operations continued and the company shut down mining altogether in 1971, not to resume until 1976 under new management (Govt. of Sierra Leone 1970, 11). How can local people fully grasp the complexities of running a large-scale mineral extraction and processing operation? Or understand risks posed by technological flaws and the use of potentially hazardous chemicals that can end up in the environment through various pathways. Add to this, the economic uncertainties of mineral global markets might result in premature mine closures. Yet, the interpretation of such events within the indigenous worldview inadvertently removes certain dimensions of blame and responsibility from mining companies and the national government.

Claims that landlord-indigene communities use sacred bush sites (genuine or fictitious) to receive compensation, extract minerals, and underscore rights to mineral resources on their lands continue. In 2014, *Awoko Newspaper* reported allegations by a government park administrator of fictitious sacred bush sites in the Sierra Leone Gola Rainforest National Park (GRNP). The article

76 CULTURE AND CONFLICTS IN SIERRA LEONE MINING

claimed that traditional authorities responsible for the management of such cultural spaces collaborated in illegal mining. They purportedly restricted the movement of official park patrols in community forest areas under the guise that sacred cultural practices were being performed (Awoko Publications, 2014). Although it is sacrilegious to interfere with sacred places under customary law, allowances may well be made in the context of indigenous land rights claims against powerful foreign mining companies and the state. These incidences illustrate the cultural dilemmas of incorporation. Marginalized people respond in different ways to asymmetrical power relations and cultural, socioeconomic, and environmental change caused by activities such as mining. The reality is that token gestures by mining companies to show cultural sensitivity do not solve the fundamental problem of cultural disruption or alienation caused by extraction. In Chapter 5, I discuss the environment as the resource base, the loss of ecological resources, and associated subsistence livelihoods related to the landlord–stranger relationship.

Chapter 5

STRANGERS, ENVIRONMENT, AND LIVELIHOODS

[...] these strangers are clearing the forest on the steep hillsides for farming and thereby denuding the watershed of the Pampana River of vegetation. The communal nature of the land tenure allows them to do this without let or hindrance, and, if anything, the local people are encouraging immigration. (Waldock et al. 1951, 79)

The Sierra Leone mining industry is over 90 years old, so there is a historical legacy of environmental deterioration in places. Mining inherently generates large volumes of waste and impacts the natural environment physically, chemically, and biologically. Unprotected mineral residue stockpiles pollute the environment and are potentially hazardous. Water systems are impacted by damming, discharge of pollutants into watercourses, sedimentation, seepage of contaminants into groundwater, and storm runoff from waste rock and tailings piles. There is more qualitative data to support this and some specific studies have quantified environmental change. Satellite imagery, tailings piles, polluted water bodies, flooding, siltation in streams and rivers, potholes, and waterborne diseases such as bilharzia, onchocerciasis, or "river blindness" and schistosomiasis (Worley Parsons Ltd. 2010).

ESHIA are standard requirements for implementing mining projects in Sierra Leone, today. Environmental laws mandate continuous monitoring for environmental and health impacts in populations around mine sites, but this is not routinely done. The early mining industry and colonial government were primarily concerned about how poor environmental management might impact economic efficiency and supply to the mineral commodity chain. The Mines Department underscored that:

The seriousness of this situation cannot be exaggerated [...] because of the destruction, from the point of view of future mining, caused by the partial extraction of the diamonds together with the mixing of the gravel with the overburden. (Govt. of Sierra Leone 1955, 3)

Methods of mineral extraction and processing, data from exploratory surveys, geology, geomorphology, weathering, and erosion can indicate areas where potentially hazardous materials may be present in the environment. The reports of the SLGS, mining company ESHIA reports, research studies, and historical narratives on the mining industry are useful sources of information, also. There are naturally occurring contaminants associated with minerals present in the environment that are released and concentrated by extractive methods. Such data are useful in helping the Environmental Protection Agency—Sierra Leone (EPA-SL) fulfill one of its responsibilities under the Environmental Protection Agency Act 2022 to "conduct environmental hazard mapping, risk and vulnerability assessment and develop a plan for environmental related disaster risk reduction" (Govt. of Sierra Leone 2022c, 15).

The drainage systems are commonly the actual mine sites for extracting alluvial deposits of minerals such as diamonds, gold, coltan, and zircon. Exploration and extraction methods include paddocking, trenching, panning, and dredging. In diamond, iron ore, and rutile areas, heavy machines excavating in drainage basins destroy riverine ecologies. Open-pit dry mining for bauxite, iron ore, and rutile destroys vegetation and topsoil reducing agricultural productivity. The extent of damage to agricultural lands and water bodies requires major capital investment for rehabilitation and reclamation. Overall, there is little systematic quantification of the extent of degradation and deteriorating environmental quality from both large-scale and artisanal operations. Much illegal mining is occurring in inaccessible forest areas of the country, which makes monitoring difficult.

From a cultural lens, strangers contribute greatly to environmental degradation and loss of livelihoods through mining. Both large-scale ventures, governed by statutes and thought of as economically efficient, and artisanal extraction embedded in traditional social relations impact the environment. The multinationals as powerful strangers use large-scale mechanical excavation methods. Although artisanal and small-scale miners employ more rudimentary technologies, activity in remote areas and under poor management degrade the environment considerably. Increasingly, locals are partnering with foreigners who bring in chemicals like mercury which have deleterious consequences that locals may not fully grasp. Further, crudely constructed dredges that locals use to hopefully improve efficiency, use gasoline and other petroleum products that also pollute the environment. While the government through legislation has increased Sierra Leonean participation in the artisanal sector, foreign partnerships may exacerbate environmental deterioration.

STRANGERS, ENVIRONMENT, AND LIVELIHOODS 79

However, I primarily focus on examples from foreign large-scale and medium-scale mining operations to emphasize the relationship between environment and culture and technology and culture. The advanced technology employed in large capital-intensive operations is a Western cultural transfer. A technological transfer is not inherently negative and can be a path to cultural evolution. However, an imbalance between technological development and the preservation of sociocultural norms and values can have negative outcomes. Massive earth-moving machines excavate and reconfigure the landscape dramatically. Dams and reservoirs alter the natural flow regime of rivers and streams. Imported, sometimes hazardous, chemicals used in blasting or mineral processing are introduced into the environment, intentionally or unintentionally. Agricultural land and ecological resources are destroyed. This level of modern and Western technology use facilitating mineral extraction also eradicates indigenous culture in places. Traditional livelihoods and ways of life can hardly be sustained in the degraded and transformed environment.

This is a cultural unequal exchange embedded in a mineral commodity chain. Western technology becomes a symbol of cultural imperialism, which explains why violent protests led by coalitions of mineworkers and communities aim to destroy company infrastructure, machinery, and vehicles. Fundamentally, provisions in state laws for large-scale operations are at odds with the traditional management of land and water resources. Mining impacts both the availability of needed resources and the cultural worldview underpinning life and livelihoods.

Environmental Deterioration from Mining

E. A. Waldock led a team of researchers, conducting a soil conservation survey in gold mining areas of northern Sierra Leone in 1948–1949. They were puzzled by strangers and landlord-indigenes collaborating in subsistence livelihoods. They did not appear to understand the long-established connection between the traditional agricultural and mining economies, and the importance of landlord–stranger reciprocities in subsistence livelihoods (Cartier and Burge 2011; Govt. of Sierra Leone 1935, 2020; Maconachie and Hilson 2011). Several present-day articles in the press alleged environmental degradation by Chinese miners sometimes partnering with Sierra Leoneans in small-scale and artisanal gold extraction operations (Embassy of the PRC 2018; Fallah-Williams 2021b; Mabey et al. 2020; Sheriff 2022). There is, thus, ambiguity in the relationships between landlord-indigenes and strangers over land use and environmental change. Partnering with certain strangers can

80   CULTURE AND CONFLICTS IN SIERRA LEONE MINING

be beneficial whether providing additional labor or access to technologies that improve mineral yields. This is cultural evolution.

Katherine Fowler-Lunn in her narrative *The Gold Missus: A Woman Prospector in Sierra Leone* described in detail the destructive nature of alluvial gold mining that she supervised in the 1930s. Alluvial deposits in the Rokel and Pampana-Jong River basins eroded from gold-bearing rock formations in the Sula Mountains and Kangari Hills. Lake Sonfon, a long-established gold mining site, is the source of the Pampana River. Extraction methods like paddocking caused large-scale deforestation. A gasoline-powered excavator operated in paddocks. Other rudimentary types of equipment used were picks, shovels, sledgehammers, cutlasses to clear forests, and headpans to carry gravel. Laborers diverted river and stream channels over many miles to provide water for washing gravel. Mine waste was dumped in forests (Fowler-Lunn 1938).

Fowler-Lunn described her use of mercury to collect gold specimens in a method called amalgamation. She mixed mercury with gold-bearing sediments or crushed ore to make a mixture called an amalgam that was stored in sealed bottles. Fowler-Lunn would then dissolve the amalgam in nitric acid. Once a week, the mix was burned in an iron bowl at Makong Camp. The enormous bonfire burned all day at the populated campsite. The mercury vaporized leaving the pure gold. At the time, there was no Miamata Convention or knowledge of mercury toxicity and its deleterious effects on the environment and human health. Fowler-Lunn who was, herself, likely unaware of the risks found it amusing that the "process always puzzled and alarmed the natives, for they felt that all their labor was going up in smoke" (Fowler-Lunn 1938, 137). Gold is still mined at Makong, and it is reasonable to assume that long-lived mercury species persist in the environment in biological, chemical, or physical media (Akiwumi 2008a). Yemen Co. Ltd., which mined lode gold underground at Baomahun in the colonial era too, also used amalgamation to recover the mineral (Govt. of Sierra Leone 1952, 4).

Today, Sierra Leone is a signatory to the Minamata Convention 2013 on mercury in the environment and health, and the EPA-SL has implemented the Development of the Minamata Initial Assessment (MIA) project and the National Action Plan (NAP) for Artisanal and Small-Scale Gold Mining (ASM) in Sierra Leone. The project findings state that mercury use is limited in gold mining. At two artisanal gold mining sites surveyed, mercury is used to process mine tailings and release gold from hard rock formations at Baomahun and Komahun. A third foreign-owned small-scale dredge mining operation at Komahun also uses mercury. The EPA-SL personnel nevertheless recognized that foreign-owned companies mining illegally may

STRANGERS, ENVIRONMENT, AND LIVELIHOODS   81

need to be monitored (Govt. of Sierra Leone 2018b). The Komahun Gold Processing Plant, in Nimikoro Chiefdom, Kono district, is an industrial-scale gold mining and processing operation considered to be the largest ever to operate in the country (Samura 2021).

Naturally occurring contaminants like arsenic derived from the mineral arsenopyrite associated with rocks containing gold in the Sula Mountains and Kangari Hills are present in the soils and water. During mineral exploration surveys in the colonial era, geologists used arsenic as a pathfinder for gold. Arsenic was concentrated in stream sediment, soils, weathered and lateritic rock, and bedrock cores from depths between 40 and 330 meters. Laboratory work detected arsenic in 4,000 samples, one with an anomalously high concentration of over 800 ppm (Wilson and Marmo 1958; Govt. of Sierra Leone 1963; Elliot 1966). A 2018 ESHIA study for AML in the same region reported high arsenic levels in springs in the Sula Mountains that feed the Mawuru River, a tributary of the Pampana. Values exceeded acceptable levels with a maximum of 0.057 mg.L^{-1}. Other potentially harmful metal species like cadmium (0.0017 mg.L^{-1}), lead (0.021 mg.L^{-1}), and selenium (0.236 mg.L^{-1}) showed high values. Groundwater leaches the metal species from iron ore bodies and other rock formations on slopes of the Sula Mountains and discharges via springs. Some well-water samples from the mining area also exceeded WHO guidelines for arsenic, barium, lead, and selenium in samples from some wells in the mine area. So both mining and natural sources of arsenic can pose health risks (WorleyParsons 2010).

The Pampana Mining Co. used a dredge in the Pampana River to increase production, which made them the largest gold producer in 1950. Rock bars in the river were blasted to create a path for the dredge (Govt. of Sierra Leone 1952). The legacy of environmental deterioration from mining in the Pampana river basin impacts communities at Lake Sonfon the headwaters and riparian communities downstream. Ecological changes caused by siltation and sedimentation limit fishing a historical livelihood in many villages. Cast net fishing widely used is hampered by turbid water. As environmental deterioration continues, it threatens the sustainability of river fishing as a cultural practice in this area. Other impacts include the loss of preferred river fish species, pride in the craft of fishing, and loss of skills and knowledge passed down through generations. Fishermen are taking on farming as an alternative livelihood out of necessity (Marcantonio and Fuentes 2020). The ESHIA for the African Minerals mine upstream documented that excavation of weathered ore deposits, and erosion of bare surfaces and waste stockpiles, would cause higher sediment loads in surface runoff and chemical contamination. Runoff and groundwater flow subsequently enter rivers like the Mawuru, a tributary of the Pampana River. The report recommended

82   CULTURE AND CONFLICTS IN SIERRA LEONE MINING

potential mitigation measures (WorleyParsons 2010). In 2019, a government coalition of the National Protected Area Authority, the Conservation Trust Fund, the National Minerals Agency, the Environment Protection Agency, and the Conservation Society of Sierra Leone arrested 12 Chinese nationals for illegal activity in the Pampana River basin. They were mining gold in Lake Sonfon, an ecologically sensitive and protected area with 156 species of birds, reptiles, and mammals (Brima 2021; The Organizer.net. 2019).

Another case study of the impacts on water systems and local livelihoods from mining is dredging for titanium minerals in southwestern Sierra Leone in sub-basins of the River Jong. I participated in ESIAs from the late 1980s to 1994 in the lease that extended over eight chiefdoms (Banta—divided into Upper Banta and Lower Banta, Banta Mokelle, Bagruwa, Bumpe, Imperi, Jong, Kpanda Kemo, Mokelle). Dredging is a massive operation that requires the construction of a series of dams on river systems to create reservoirs that flood vast areas and destroy fertile agricultural lands and topsoil. Rutile and ilmenite, ores of titanium and zircon, are important foreign exchange earners for Sierra Leone. The Sierra Rutile Agreement permits the company:

> To dig, widen and deepen channels in rivers, streams and watercourses as necessary [...] to use water from any natural watercourse and to return the same, together with mining spoils to that watercourse provided no poisonous or noxious matter not present in the intake water is discharged therein [...] to divert streams, to build temporary dams and to impound water to secure the supply of water needed for mining operations. (Govt. of Sierra Leone 2002)

Preparation alters the landscape in concentrated areas where the deposits lie and involves extensive manipulation of river systems and the acquisition of adjacent lands (see Figure 5.1). Figure 5.2 compares a premining image from 1964 and the transformed landscape comprising a mosaic of reservoirs, tailings, cleared areas, vegetation patches, and interspersed villages in 1990 (Akiwumi and Butler 2008b; Akiwumi et al. 1990; Lamin et al. 1991). Dams on sub-basins of the Jong and Gbangbaia Rivers created reservoirs, locally called dredge ponds, where the dredge and wet plant operate as shown in Figure 5.2. Another dredge, *Solondo*, was under construction in 2005 (Figure 5.3). Reservoir construction involves land clearing, sometimes including village relocation. Spillways control water levels so that the dredge can float. Large volumes of tailings and slimes are dumped in and around the reservoirs. Road networks transport machinery, people, and mineral ore. Figure 5.3 is a picture of the Solondo dredge under construction in 2005 and Figure 5.4 shows the dredge and wet plant on Lanti Pond in the same

STRANGERS, ENVIRONMENT, AND LIVELIHOODS   83

Figure 5.1 Landscape of ponds, sand tailings, and slimes from rutile mining, 2005.

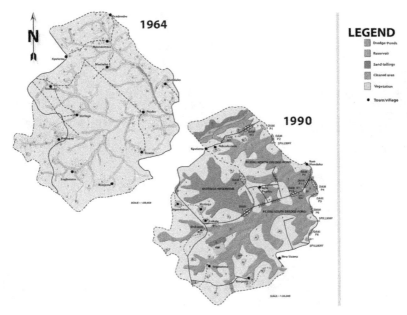

Figure 5.2 Land use changes from rutile dredging, 1964–1990.

Figure 5.3 Solondo dredge under construction, 2005.

Figure 5.4 Dredge and wet plant on Lanti deposit.

Figure 5.5 Rutile ore ready for shipment.

year. Figure 5.5 presents rutile ore loaded in a barge and ready for shipment. Subsistence livelihoods continue in the degraded landscape as shown in Figures 5.6 and 5.7.

When the rutile company reprocessed tailings stockpiles for zircon from 1990 to 1991, some reagents used in the Zircon Wet Plant were amines, sodium hydroxide, sulfuric acid, hydrochloric acid, and hydrogen fluoride. These chemicals were measured in effluent streams and well water during an

Figure 5.6 Cassava cultivation on mine tailings, Moyamba District.

Figure 5.7 Brick making using sand tailings and slimes.

STRANGERS, ENVIRONMENT, AND LIVELIHOODS 87

Environmental Impact Assessment (EIA). Another EIA in 2001 by Knight Piesold determined that overall, surface and groundwater quality, quantity, and supply were of concern. Seepage water beneath the embankments at the mined-out Bamba-Belebu dredge pond was remarkably acidic. Two historic solid waste landfills were a likely risk to local groundwater contamination though no data was available. It was necessary to carry out remediation to effectively contain mine wastes that would necessitate maintaining embankments on dams. There was evidence of past poor waste management such as disposing of fuels, oils, solvents, and other hazardous wastes in the bush. Nonmaintenance of the mine during the 10-year rebel war was also a factor in the problem of unlabeled leaking drums containing unknown chemicals. Strong recommendations were made for monitoring and reporting on waste disposal and mitigation measures going forward. The report concluded that conditions at the mine site were not in compliance with the provisions of the law (Knight Piesold 2001; Sannoh and Squire 1994; Squire 1993).

Other quality concerns include radiation as background levels of radioactivity were measured in the mining area during the exploration phase and more recently in ore stockpiles near the Plant Site. This derives from the radioactive mineral monazite associated with the rutile and ilmenite. Further, eight million tons of ore produce 200,000 tons of rutile and ilmenite combined. So over the many years of mining, a tremendous volume of waste material has been produced. Mine waste is a mixture of lateritic rock fragments, sands, and finer tailings, which is dumped back into dredge ponds or discarded around the periphery as sand tailings and rock heaps. Dry mining using large excavators also moves large volumes of earthen material and exposes bare areas to surface runoff. Sediment is carried into nearby water bodies (Keili 1993; Knight Piesold and Co. 2001; Mckenzie 1963).

Water availability and deteriorating water quality for communities are major conflict issues. There are numerous examples of water conflicts over the history of Sierra Leone mining. I share some examples. In 1969, distressed Chiefdom leaders petitioned the Prime Minister of Sierra Leone to intervene in an involuntary relocation of Bongema village, Kono District. Company excavation equipment dumped earth and uprooted trees in their drinking water supply source. In bewilderment, they asked: Are you going to allow this evil company to transgress against the natural laws of human existence? What shall we drink now? (Conteh 1979, 204). The protest was unsuccessful as mining occurred there and the landlord-indigenes had to settle for compensation.

As recently as December 2022 also in Kono District, Amnesty International reported on water quality issues in boreholes built by Meya Mining in the

88   CULTURE AND CONFLICTS IN SIERRA LEONE MINING

relocated Koaquima village community. The levels of nitrates in two water samples exceeded the World Health Organization safe levels of 50 mg.L^{-1} measured at 110 mg.L^{-1} and 120 mg.L^{-1}. Following the intervention by Amnesty International, the company installed water filtration and purification systems to reduce nitrate concentrations. Amnesty reminded the company that the United Nations Guiding Principles on Business and Human Rights emphasize that "communities must give their prior consent for all forms of resource exploitation on their traditional lands and must also benefit accordingly" (Amnesty International 2022).

Other times, perceptions of deteriorating water quality are colored by local understandings. Water analysis on a village well revealed extremely acidic conditions and the presence of chemicals used in the mining process (Squire 1994; Squire and Sannoh 1993). A villager attributed the bad taste and smell to a poison called *lasmami* that allegedly targets a particular individual. In this case, the target was a mine employee, who was a political aspirant.

Women Own the Water—Cultural Disruption and Scoop-Net Fishing

Village locations are close to water bodies (rivers, streams, and swamps) for domestic water supply and livelihoods. Sites often coincide with ancient alluvial deposits that might be mineral bearing. In these cases, companies relocate villages to access mineral resources or facilitate mining operations. Certain customary water-based livelihoods are destroyed, including recessional farming and swamp rice cultivation. Riparian and swamp forests provide a variety of products such as construction materials (building poles and raffia for matting and roofing) and edible and medicinal plants. Fishing is an important livelihood. Fishing and hunting rights belong to chiefdoms, and landowners can hunt or fish anywhere, although a token gift is expected when a stream flows through someone's yard or farm. Younger kin and strangers need permission from members of land-holding families to fish. There are legal prohibitions under customary law against damming of rivers as the process disrupts fish breeding cycles and deprives upstream users of water (Fenton 1948; Wohlwend 1978).

Scoop-net fishing in the dry season when river levels are low is women's work. They wade in the water and place their relatively small *mbembei* and *fele* nets close to the banks to catch fish trapped in pockets or small pools. During field surveys, our Environmental and Scientific Consulting Group (ESCG) encountered women trying to scoop-net fish downstream of dams. The standard complaint was that increased seepage beneath dams was changing the seasonal flow regimes of streams. Water levels

Figure 5.8 Women scoop-net fishing in mined-out Mogbwemo dredge pond.

in the lower reaches of rivers/streams were too high to allow this shallow-water fishing method. Our consultancy, made up of scientists and unaware of the sociocultural context of female fishing, simply recorded the problem of elevated water levels affecting fishing in a consultancy report to the mining company. The company management addressed the issue by stocking the mined-out Mogbwemo dredge pond with Tilapia fingerlings to provide fish for villagers. Villagers complained about the type of fish as it was unfamiliar (Figure 5.8).

On further investigation, we found out that what seemed like a straightforward problem of the availability of fish had huge implications for gender social relations among the Mende landlord-indigenes.

90 CULTURE AND CONFLICTS IN SIERRA LEONE MINING

Melissa Leach in her 1994 publication "Rainforest Relations: Resource Use among the Mende of Gola, Sierra Leone" and Marianne Ferme (2000) in "The Underneath of Things: Violence and the Every Day in Sierra Leone" extensively elaborate on gender relations, water, and fishing in Mende culture. In fact, the missionary George E. Thompson documented groups of young girls scoop-net fishing in nineteenth-century Mendi country (Thompson 1852).

The *mbembei* and the basket to carry fish (*piye*) are powerful female symbols. Weaving nets is often a joint social activity. Young girls acquire their nets following initiation in Sande and this is symbolic of their achieving adult status. Scoop nets are individually owned unlike the larger nets used by men in communal societies. The *mbembei* is used by one person or the larger *fele* by two people. Weaving scoop nets is a source of female pride because the art form requires more advanced technical skills than producing larger male fishing nets.

In Sande, there is symbolism attached to scoop nets, water, and childbirth where the scoop net is analogous to the womb capable of both containment and release. The fishing environment is a women's space where women bond and share concerns and camaraderie. Women fish in groups comprising kin and close friends. Mende emphasizes bonds and close ties between women by pointing to the fact that "they go fishing together." Men respect this female space and choose not to participate in women's fishing expeditions although there are no set restrictions. They typically revere the association of the activity with Sande—a "women's secret society" (Ferme 2000; Leach 1994).

The mine closed down in 1995 because of the RUF/SL rebel incursion in Sierra Leone. The closure affected the livelihoods of many communities dependent on the mine. The dredge ponds, which had caused conflicts in the past between communities and the company, were now providing income for local people and unemployed mine workers through fishing. Fish had always contributed to domestic consumption and provided income in the marketplace for women. Raised water levels in dredge ponds, however, now facilitated deepwater fishing with gill nets and canoes, employed by men. Women were thus marginalized to the peripheral areas of dredge ponds. The new fishing arrangements also invalidated traditional sanctions (*sawa*) administered by village chiefs and elders to protect fish-breeding grounds at certain times of the year.

A few fishermen agreed that dams had created reservoirs deep enough for them to fish profitably year-round. One or two were not in favor of draining dredge ponds as a rehabilitation option. At Kpetema village located approximately 150 meters from the Mogbwemo dredge pond, I spoke with six women about the issue of fishing. One of them, a village elder about 80 years old, was the Sande leader (*Sowei*) head of Sande and the local midwife. She was weaving a scoop net that would take her two to three weeks to complete. Another was a long-time stranger who had moved to the area with her now-deceased husband, a mine employee in 1968.

All of the women confirmed the changing dynamics in fishing caused by damming rivers. Men had the advantage of going out into deeper water with their canoes and large gill nets. They would disturb the water's surface to attract fish toward the center. The women sometimes fished late at night when the water was still. They were not concerned about safety because "women own the water" according to a male village resident. He was alluding to the intimate relationship between members of Sande and water bodies. The water spirit, Tingoi, lives in "the holiest of domains, deep waters and out at sea or in big rivers and ponds" (Boone (1986, 129).

Another constraint related to female fishing was the scarcity of the specific plant material used to construct the frames and weave the mesh in the scoop nets. The dredge ponds submerged riparian vegetation destroying many useful tree species and grasses used as fiber, rope, matting, and construction. They recognized that they might soon have to rely on imported synthetic fibers and netting to make scoop nets. They further recognized the consequences for the craftsmanship and livelihood of net makers, but adjustments had to be made (Akiwumi 2006).

Mining Regulations and Cultural Sensitivity

There was limited environmental awareness by actors in the early mining industry as illustrated by mercury use. Some mining ordinances and rules did contain provisions for environmental management and monitoring and pollution control. They were sometimes sensitive to landholders and other times ambiguous and generally poorly implemented. The Minerals Amendment Ordinance, 1947 (No. 28 of 1947) required the holder of an alluvial gold mining license "to pay compensation to the owner for any loss of economic trees or crops caused by mining operations" (Govt. of Sierra Leone 1949, 5). A soil conservation survey of Sierra Leone in 1948–1949 addressed land degradation and land reclamation in gold mining areas. It recommended leveling overburden and tailings and infilling excavations. The report even proposed that "where mining operations cannot pay for reasonable rehabilitation of the land, mining should be regarded as uneconomic and not permitted" (Waldock et al. 1951, 79). This has proved to be a tall order in a country where more than half of the surface area is covered in mine leases and illicit mining is rampant.

92 CULTURE AND CONFLICTS IN SIERRA LEONE MINING

A "Safe Mining" section was added to the General Mineral Rules in 1953. Under the Minerals (Safe Mining) Rules, a provision addressed the "safe disposal of waste":

> Any water containing poisonous or injurious chemical solutions and situated in any mining area shall be effectively fenced off to prevent inadvertent access thereto and a notice board shall be placed in a conspicuous position adjacent thereto to warn persons against making use of such water. (Govt. of Sierra Leone 1960b, 1749)

This statement was absurd considering many of those likely to be affected could not read the English language. A recent mining company ESHIA similarly recommended warning signs but in the local language of the area (SRK Consulting 2018b). The problem with this is that many indigenous languages are unwritten.

An Economic Commission of Africa (ECA) review of mining legislation and agreements in Sierra Leone shortly after independence addressed "the extent to which the exploitation of mineral resources could imperil agricultural or forestry interests or lead to industrial pollution and the steps which the company can effectively take to avoid or compensate for such losses" (UNECA, 1969, 10).

Under the current Environment Protection Agency Act 2022, the EPA-SL is the focal institution for all issues concerning the environment. Companies must conduct an EIA. Pollution control and prevention and land reclamation and rehabilitation are legal requirements for mining companies. Rehabilitation goals include restoring impacted land and water resources and preventing such deleterious offsite environmental consequences as health and safety hazards to surrounding populations. An EIA should contain information on "social, economic and cultural effects that the project is likely to have on people and society" (Govt. of Sierra Leone 2022c, 25). The National Environment Compliance and Enforcement Coordination Committee is made up of a diverse group working collaboratively to ensure the enforcement of environmental laws and regulations. Scarce resources limit adequate monitoring of the activities of companies for compliance. However, in 2019, Sierra Leone became one of several African countries in the Africa Regional Data Cube. The United States NASA is helping countries monitor illegal mining and environmental degradation by providing access to satellite imagery and help with analyzing data (Jacket Media Co. 2021).

In terms of engaging traditional authority in an expanding mineral sector, there is a representative of the Council of Paramount Chiefs on the Minerals Advisory Board but not on the EPA Advisory Board or the National

Environment Compliance and Enforcement Coordination Committee. However, every chiefdom has a Chiefdom Environment Committee comprising the Paramount Chief, Section Chiefs, the chiefdom Councilor, Chiefdom Youth Leaders, Chiefdom Women's Leaders, the President, the Interreligious Council of Sierra Leone, and a representative of the Chiefdom Mines Committee. The committee, however, receives some directives from the Executive Director of EPA-SL such as assigning chiefdom areas as bush or forest and for water conservation, fishing, food production, and ecotourism. These responsibilities are a carryover from the colonial Tribal Authorities Ordinance of 1938 where the Paramount Chiefs and Tribal Authorities had similar functions. With oversight from the Governor, chiefdom leadership was to prevent the pollution of water sources and obstruction of water courses, and prohibit, restrict, or regulate cutting down or destroying trees. Additionally, they were to prohibit, restrict, or regulate the burning of bush or grass for farming and promote the cultivation of food crops for communities.

One of the biggest challenges around mining and environmental legislation is local understanding and perception. In the rutile lease, for example, where environmental destruction is easily visible, there is much anger against the mining company as a powerful stranger appropriating land and water. In December 2009, a civil society group, The Children's Welfare and Community Development Programme (CWADEP), partnered with the United Kingdom Department of International Development's program on Enhancing the Interaction and Interface between Civil Society and the State (DfID-ENCISS) and CARE Sierra Leone to host a workshop at the rutile mine. The event was open to the public and the agenda was to popularize the rutile agreement, assess whether the then pending Mines and Mineral Act of 2009 reflected the wishes of the people, and address the roles and responsibilities of the company, government, chiefs, local councils, and civil society in mining law reform.

Some participants expressed grievances over land rights and accused the mining company of taking their lands. Another participant summarized feelings about environmental degradation and the loss of cultural heritage sites: "We are living as strangers in our own land, without the right to be involved in negotiations before our fertile agricultural lands are leased out to the company" (Sierra Express Media 2009). A company representative at the workshop maintained that the company is law abiding and operates within the terms of its signed lease agreement with the national government.

This is true. However, scrutiny of the Sierra Rutile Agreement reveals inherent conflicts that challenge the prospect of conflict resolution. Landlord-indigene communities do not fully grasp the extent of rights granted to

94 CULTURE AND CONFLICTS IN SIERRA LEONE MINING

mining companies through state laws. The Agreement reinforced the right of the National Government to override traditional authority:

> [...] the Government shall indemnify the Company against all claims of any owners or occupiers [of land] (including the Chiefdom Councilors) in respect of a Prospecting Area other than compensation claims already agreed upon.

According to the law, in any disagreement with landowners, the government representative will make the final decision on the amount of compensation. Further, compensation rates will not factor in the long-term degradation of land caused by disturbing topsoil and intermixing it with subsoil strata, an inevitable result of the mining operations. This right to degrade soils has major implications for communities where subsistence agriculture is the main livelihood. The question of land for agriculture in the future came up frequently in company–community discussions of the SRL Mine Closure Plan (Govt. of Sierra Leone 2002, 13; SRK 2018b).

This clause about the government indemnifying the company is standard in special agreements dating back to the Tonkolili Agreement of 1933. This agreement went as far as to state that if any owner or occupier refused to give up their land, the police or Magistrate's Court would forcefully acquire it for the company. Another persistent and problematic clause in agreements is that mining companies can relinquish any area within a Prospecting License or acquire additional areas outside but contiguous with the Prospecting Area at any time. Under these circumstances, the approval of the Director of Mines "shall not be unreasonably withheld" (Govt. of Sierra Leone 2002, 13–14). Sierra Rutile exercised this right in November 2006 when it returned 26,625 acres of once-leased land to the Chiefdom Councilors. The company needed to streamline its operations because it incurred huge financial losses to infrastructure and mine closure during the war. One way was to reduce the acreage of land it was paying rent on. Landowners accustomed to receiving surface rent payments were angry over the loss of revenue from lands excluded. Protests included roadblocks to prevent mining operations (Mansaray 2006; Winnebah 2006). This was a time of hardship for communities as the mine was shut down in 1995 because of the RUF/SL for 10 years. There were few mine jobs and associated economic opportunities. Traditional farming was not a livelihood option in the degraded landscape or within any leased space.

Another example of a companies' right to acquire and relinquish land under lease involved the exploration lease that SLDC held in the Tonkolili District in the colonial era. It was a designated closed area meaning no one including landlord-indigenes could breach the boundaries for any reason. The lease was placed on a care and maintenance basis for some time and the local people asked to regain some of the lands within for farming. The company agreed to all areas except on the slopes of Simbili and Marampon villages "in the interests and the safety of the people themselves" (Govt. of Sierra Leone 1962, 13). These villages were long situated on hilltops within the Sula Mountain range, the drainage divide between the Pampana and Rokel Rivers. The landlord-indigenes had historically farmed the slopes and mined gold in the springfed streams that flow on the eastern slopes of Simbili and safety was not a concern. However, two of the four major iron ore bodies Simbili, Marampon, Numbara, and Kasafoni mapped out during survey work lay under these two villages (Mining Technology 2021). This fact and gold mining by locals were likely the reasons behind prohibiting any activity at these locations. The SLDC did have a supplementary agreement to also prospect for gold within the lease (The Sierra Leone Web 2023).

Updated laws guided by international best practices in the mining industry address community development as an important part of sustainable development based on mineral revenue. The Mines and Minerals Development Act 2022 requires mining companies to have Community Development Agreements (CDA) with host communities. The Act contains broad statements such as to "ensure that the development of the minerals sector is achieved in ways that are economically beneficial, socially responsible and will protect the environment." It also states that local communities will be protected from the impacts of mining operations on their livelihoods and infrastructure, and benefit from land rent charges imposed on mine operators by the landowners.

At the local level of governance within communities, groups are emerging to address concerns regarding the substantial changes in the traditional culture and the degradation of the environment caused by mining operations. These include the community more broadly but also women and youth groups. Increasingly, these groups build alliances with local and global civil society organizations to address environmental and social concerns about mining. Some examples of active community organizations are the Land Owners Federation and Community Advocacy and Development Project (CADEP) in the rutile area, the Marginalized Affected Property Owners (MAPO) from Gbense and Tankoro chiefdoms in Kono District, and Save Lake Sonfon of Sierra Leone. Some supporting national and international organizations are the Sierra Leonean NGOs Network Movement for Justice and Development (NMJD) and Women on Mining and Extractive—Sierra Leone (WOME-SL); Amnesty International, Global GreenGrant, and EarthRights International (U.S). Descendants of Lunsar wrote an open letter to London Mining in 2013 expressing concerns about conditions in their communities caused by iron ore extraction (The Patriotic Vanguard 2013a, 2013b).

96 CULTURE AND CONFLICTS IN SIERRA LEONE MINING

Supporting organizations sometimes assist with filing lawsuits against companies in countries like the United States or the United Kingdom or regionally at the ECOWAS Court of Justice in Abuja, Nigeria (Black 2022). In 2020, 15 individuals from Koidu took the diamond mining company Octea Group/BSG Resources to court in Freetown for environmental deterioration. The group leader explained:

> We're suing Octea for forcibly taking our people's land pushing us from our homes, burying our farmland under rubble and degrading community water sources. While we suffer, they undercompensate affected families and fail to provide the community support payments that they promised.

A coalition of civil society groups, the Network Movement for Justice and Development (NMJD), Advocates for Community Alternatives (ACA), and C & J Partners helped draw attention to the case (KPCSC 2020). While power dynamics are not the focus of this work, the challenges landlord-indigene face over land rights is embedded in unequal power relations operating at several scales: globally, nationally, and locally at the mine site and within landlord-indigene communities, and their households due to the presence of strangers.

Chapter 6

RACE, ETHNICITY, CLASS, AND GENDER IN MINING

> The mining company and the expatriate community represent an entirely different social world from that of Mogbwemo, but since they are involved in the same economic system, there is constant feedback between them.[...] Relationships between them, however, still basically revolve round superior-subordinate relations. (Labi 1972, 48)

In the colonial era, government geologists and mining engineers, and professionals and management at mining companies were predominantly Caucasian while Africans worked as laborers. The permanent mining enclave today is more racially and ethnically diverse, not a melting pot but rather a bubbling cauldron. Traditional structures wrestle with new hierarchical arrangements that support capital-intensive and technologically advanced extractive operations. Top management of foreign companies is typically expatriate, largely Caucasian, but today, including Chinese. Managers make up a small percentage of the workforce. Expatriate employees are hired under a different and higher salary scale than well-qualified Sierra Leonean or other African counterparts for equal or greater work. These spaces are plagued by issues like racial and class discrimination, ethnic strife, gender marginalization, and related unrest.

During the early years of mining in Sierra Leone, there was an influx of job seekers. An early photograph taken by Fowler-Lunn (1938, 128–129) in 1931 at Makong showed a six a.m. roll call with close to 300 people seeking employment as labor for the day. Figure 6.1 similarly shows labor outside the Sierra Rutile Plant Site seeking work in 2005. By 1963, Sierra Leone had the highest percentage of young men, out of the total male population giving up farming for mine employment compared to other West African mining economies. The SLDC employed about 5,000 men in 1931 at the iron ore mine at Marampa. When the Mining Wages Board of Sierra Leone introduced new wage policies in 1945 under the Wages Board Ordinance and as the company adopted labor-saving techniques, it gradually

Figure 6.1 Wage labor at plant site, SRL Mine, 2005.

reduced its wage labor workforce. The numbers decreased from 4,195 in 1940 to 2,692 in 1960 and to 2,500 in 1975 (Clark 1966; Saylors 1967). This naturally affected workers now dependent on a new livelihood and their families. Tension occurred in mineworker households because the pay did not cover the many responsibilities. The inflation in mining areas meant the cost of food was high. Companies would supply staple foodstuffs like rice at subsidized prices for workers. The SLST in 1952 also subsidized palm oil and when the cost of local fish was high imported cured herrings for workers (Govt. of Sierra Leone 1954, 4). Women in households found alternative livelihoods to supplement household income. Women are oftentimes under the impression that their husbands must make decent money since they work for a company.

In the early colonial years, life at the mines was hard and dangerous work. Accidents occurred frequently and the Mines Department kept meticulous records of injuries and death including causes that were reported in the annual reports. The detailed reporting of injuries in the mines report slowed down following Independence in 1961. There is a history of strikes by disgruntled Sierra Leonean mineworkers over a variety of issues including low wages. Oftentimes, landlord-indigenes and strangers band together with workers

RACE, ETHNICITY, CLASS, AND GENDER IN MINING   99

in protest against the mining companies. Other conflicts linked to historic ethnic differences arise periodically among hired wage labor strangers. There are grievances at other scales down to the level of the chiefdom, household, and family encompassing class and gender dynamics. Landlord-indigenes sometimes see their chiefs as complicit with the companies, and the national government, and selected stranger groups to their disadvantage.

Racial discrimination incidences are a lingering issue at mines dating back to the fully segregated camps in colonial times. Companies build walled living quarters, locally known as reservations, with developed world living conditions for expatriates and since Independence senior-level Sierra Leonean employees. Satellite dishes, air conditioning, electricity, water, and furnished housing contrast surrounding rural villages. The SLST had African staff quarters and Labor camps (Govt. of Sierra Leone 1952). The majority of unskilled employees at mines (landlord-indigenes and strangers) and their dependents live in traditional villages and boom towns, with a lack of basic amenities like water and electricity. These amenities are also inadequate in other parts of the country, including in large cities, but the contrast is palpable at the scale of the mining enclave.

At DELCO at Marampa, the expatriates' living quarters were strategically located a good distance from the African quarters so as not to "endanger the health of the European camp owing to the direction of the prevailing wind." The camp was also fenced and heavily guarded (Hauser 2013, 59; Sierra Leone Development Co Ltd 1944). The Club House and Marampa Golf Club were exclusively for expatriate employees. An Austrian company ran the mine from 1983 to 85 and continued patterns and policies that were first established by SLDC Ltd. In this European, specifically Austrian enclave, portraits of the Austrian chancellor Bruno Kreisky were put on display in official buildings at the mine. An Austrian chef was brought to Sierra Leone to provide Austrian meals at the Senior Staff Club. There was a special school for Austrian children. Many of the Austrians considered themselves working-class people who were unfamiliar with being treated as elites and having domestic servants. The class differences created at the mine were based solely on race. However, many Austrians went out of their way to cultivate a personal relationship with their domestic help (Hauser 2013).

In the colonial period, companies built "native" labor camps or villages for Africans and separated workers by ethnicity according to the Mines Department reports. The SLST camps had traditional kitchens, latrines, and bathhouses. The camps were close to areas being worked at any given point in time such as Bandafayi, Gaiya, Koidu, Kwakwayi, Masundu, and Motema (ex. Govt. of Sierra Leone 1938, 1948, 1949, 1957). The labor housing schemes at SLDC iron ore mines at Marampa and Farangbaia and

100   CULTURE AND CONFLICTS IN SIERRA LEONE MINING

Maroc Co. gold camps also segregated workers in hamlets by ethnic group as well. Segregation was intended to contain historic tensions between groups and any landlord-indigene and stranger animosities. Fowler-Lunn described how Mende strangers and Temne hosts took sides in a fight between a Mende petty trader selling salt to a Temne at what was considered an exorbitant price at Makong. The Mende threatened to burn down Temne huts. Following the incident, the Marco Co. mine management built a labor camp for the workers to separate them from the landlord-indigene villagers. Within the camp, they further separated the workers according to ethnic groups "for the peace of the mine" (Fowler-Lunn 1938, 148). Thus, over a matter as simple as the price of salt, deep-seated tensions and frustrations over rights and place revealed themselves through near-violent confrontation.

Another race issue was the derogatory way that whites often treated Africans. The colonial mindset that Africans were primitive and backward was reflected in attitudes at the mines. Even some Caucasian visitors sometimes expressed disgust at the way white supervisors treated African employees. Robert Steel, an Oxford graduate, visited Sierra Leone to conduct a geographical survey with a focus on population and land use. He found the treatment of Africans by white miners at Marampa appalling and was ashamed of being an Englishman as he witnessed the physical and verbal abuse. Steel disagreed "violently" with the attitude of mine management at the Sakasakala mine camp on Lake Sonfon toward the black man (Steel 2001, 53).

Katherine Fowler-Lunn, an American, gave an insider's view on racism at the early 1930s Maroc gold mines. Her 1938 narrative is very insightful and reminiscent of the American Wild West. She described prospectors, companies and adventurers staking claims, primitive overcrowded mine camps, and very poor overall treatment of the African wage laborers working 12-hour shifts. She hoped that the government would intervene with proper supervision and institute "real mining laws." She could foresee the backlash from the poor treatment of African workers writing:

> One could almost feel the boiling hatred of many of the natives. It was only a matter of time before someone would come along and rouse the blacks to turn upon their masters. Before long the miner would have to listen to those who outnumbered him so heavily. The time was coming soon when the natives would realize that these whites were bleeding them of their natural riches. (Fowler-Lunn 1938, 148)

Her prediction came true when in 1932 "minor uprisings, arguments and fights" eventually erupted into a major revolt when several hundred armed mineworkers attacked the compound housing the three white employees

RACE, ETHNICITY, CLASS, AND GENDER IN MINING 101

at Makong. The three white managers barricaded themselves indoors, making crude trench bombs to protect themselves. The Paramount Chief of the chiefdom where the mine was located traveled five miles from his headquarters at Makali to Makong to try and contain the situation but with little success. The District Commissioner at Makeni, the headquarters town of Tonkolili District, arrived two and a half days later with a contingent of soldiers to reestablish law and order. The leaders were arrested, fined, and given jail sentences. The official Mines Department report of the incident was a modified version that downplayed the involvement of mine workers, stating:

> A small band of agitators going from place to place created some minor disturbances at some of the gold mining camps, but after rioting and intimidating labour and townspeople in October they were dealt with finally and since then no more troubles have arisen. (Govt. of Sierra Leone 1934, 12)

Some white expatriates were conflicted between their preconceived racist views on Africa and Africans and their observations on the ground. Generally, they subscribed to the imperialistic views of the time that civilizing and modernizing Africans was an ultimate goal. At the same time, they sympathized with the effects of cultural imperialism on native peoples and appreciated their simple lives free of the stressors of modern industrialized living (Mitchell 2002; Steel 2001). Fowler-Lunn was impressed by the African knowledge of iron ore mining and ore processing but was disappointed that the local people did not share this knowledge with her. She knew that the colonial government at some point banned this long-established iron ore industry to stop the making of weapons "in the interest of peace" (1938, 94). This policy impacted the production of farming tools and household utensils. The government did not consider the effects of this decision on the important subsistence livelihoods of artisanal mining and farming. Neither did they consider the loss of status for the blacksmith in traditional society because he makes and repairs farming and hunting tools for rural communities' subsistence livelihoods. When she came upon a primitive kiln for processing low-grade iron ore, she informed the chief of the area and sent him a piece of higher-grade ore she had found during exploration work. Essentially, a slap in his face she admitted.

There are many other examples of strikes at mines in the colonial era reported in the Mines Department reports. Some examples are a 10-day strike at SLST in 1951 (Govt. of Sierra Leone 1953, 4), and two more in January and August 1959; a 10-day unofficial strike in 1959 (Govt. of Sierra Leone 1960a, 15) followed by a two-day strike in 1960 at SLDC iron ore mine at Farangbaia over labor conditions (Govt. of Sierra Leone 1961, 20). At one

102   CULTURE AND CONFLICTS IN SIERRA LEONE MINING

point, the SLDC brought in a European Labor Officer in 1951 to facilitate good industrial relations (Govt. of Sierra Leone 1953, 5). However, strikes continue into the postcolonial period (Reuters 2018) and labor intimidation in mines is real. A Caucasian expatriate manager told his African workers they could choose between his protection or "protection offered by the union." Benefits he could offer included monetary loans, car rides to and from work sites, and lunch breaks (Labi 1972, 51).

Strikes and uprisings have continued into the postcolonial period over the same issues including racial discrimination. The ambivalent relationship between landlords and strangers is evident during strikes. They often form alliances during uprisings against companies and the government. In 1995, during the RUF/SL war, rebels and local people attacked the SRL mine. They burnt down the administrative building, looted and vandalized company accommodations, and destroyed other company property. Three expatriates and two Sierra Leonean personnel were abducted but later released. In December 2007, an uprising occurred at Koidu Holdings led by 1,000 illicit miners. They were joined by angry landlord-indigenes suffering the effects of the blasting of kimberlite rock for diamonds. Another grievance was the poorly planned village relocations. Communities were dissatisfied with the response of the national government and Koidu Holdings management to their frequently reported concerns. Altogether, some 3,400 protestors with weapons like knives, rocks, spades, and sticks invaded the mine site looting and damaging company property. A protestor was killed by security forces (Heilmann 2007). More recently, in December 2012, another strike at Koidu Holdings resulted in violence and two dead. Workers were aggrieved by racist treatment by expatriate supervisors. Strikers at AML had similar complaints of racism during an April 2012 strike where the police used guns and tear gas to disperse the crowds of local people and workers (Human Rights Watch 2014).

We Are the People Here: Land Rights, Hiring Practices, and CSR

Another cultural challenge is the periodic protests by community leaders and young people with ancestral rights to land demanding jobs from the companies operating in their area. As landowners, surface rent payment alone is inadequate compensation because there are few other benefits from a company's use of their lands. If the land that sustained their traditional livelihoods for generations is given over to a new livelihood, then they should have first rights to new opportunities. In 2008, the chief of a town in a mining area raised the issue of landlord-indigenes of the chiefdom not being hired at the company. He felt the mine was a mixed blessing: "We are

RACE, ETHNICITY, CLASS, AND GENDER IN MINING   103

happy the mine is here, but we don't feel a part of the mine" (Seibure and Hill 2008). In the traditional worldview, people belong to a place not the other way round.

New class structures created by mining marginalize the landlord–stranger institution. In the mines, expatriates, professional Africans, labor gang leaders, security officers, foremen, supporters, license holders, and mineral dealers are all new influential actors. The loss of land to mining companies marginalizes customary leaders and elites (chiefs, blacksmiths, and spiritual leaders) whose status is based on land management. Observers raise the issue of class disparity between company employees and landowners in mining communities. An observer compared life in a mining area to "the animal farm situation wherein the class distinction is so glaring that one begins to wonder whether the indigenes whose land is being exploited matter at all" (Sierra Express Media 2009).

Traditional leaders sometimes adapt to changing circumstances and will accept low-wage employment at a mine. Other chiefs will not take a company job because it lowers their traditional leadership roles and status. After all, this is their land and they will not be treated like strangers. Chiefs might not have the required level of Western education for more senior or specialized positions within a company. Thus, they run the risk of ending up in a subordinate rank to their subjects holding higher positions, which is humiliating. Two chiefs were allegedly ridiculed by some subjects behind closed doors for accepting employment at a mine (Labi 1972).

To be hired in a position above wage labor, mine employees must have a Western education up to at least the West African Senior School Certificate. Companies promise and sometimes provide training to increase job opportunities for Sierra Leoneans in the industry. For instance, a Trade Training Center opened in April 1957 that trained 55 mechanical and electrical students and 85 for construction work. There was also The New Mining School that prepared 11 trainees for admission to university in the United Kingdom to earn degrees that would qualify them for senior positions with the company. Similarly, the DELCO Scholars Program sent students abroad, enrolled them in overseas correspondence courses and offered tutorials (Govt. of Sierra Leone 1961, 1962; SRK Consulting 2018a).

Companies try to reason with traditional authorities and disgruntled youth demanding jobs simply because they are from the landowning communities. While they do try to give priority to landowners, other qualified Sierra Leoneans are entitled to compete for job opportunities in mining areas based on merit (Awoko Publications 2010b). Also for technologically advanced operations, specialized training is required. The SRL brings in specialized labor for particular phases of its operations.

104   CULTURE AND CONFLICTS IN SIERRA LEONE MINING

In 2008, OCI, contractors in dredge operations, a Malaysian-based company, brought 125 Malaysians to build and maintain dredges and housed them in the "Malaysian compound" with their cook and other culturally appropriate amenities (Meeting at SRL, May 2008). Similarly, the team involved in the infrastructure development for dry mining at Gangama and Gbeni from 2013 to 2019 comprised 81 expatriates from South Africa and Ghana and 34 Sierra Leoneans (SRK Consulting 2018a).

The SRL has programs to support education and increase job prospects for locals and Sierra Leoneans, more broadly. The Sierra Rutile Educational Programme provides scholarships for primary and secondary school children who are indigenous to the five chiefdoms in which the company operates. In addition, the Ruby Rose Educational Resource Centre supports education programs. There is also a Sierra Rutile Internship Programme for college students from Fourah Bay College, Njala University, and a funded technical institute, the Jackson and Devon Anderson Technical Institute (JADA). Students intern in various fields like finance and management, geology, information technology, and mining engineering. These educational opportunities, notwithstanding, the company emphasizes that there are only a limited number of jobs available. But based on deeply held cultural beliefs, the expectation by landlord-indigenes to be prioritized in hiring persists. This was evident in posts on the company's LinkedIn page in response to news that the Sembehun Project when developed would extend the life of the company's operations and, therefore, job opportunities. Examples of comments included "I am a son of the soil" and "do employ people that originated from the SRL communities" (Sierra Rutile LinkedIn 2023a, 2023b). However, there is much debate as to whether the mining industry has given rise to tangible development overall. International Best Practices call for corporate social responsibility (CSR). Land legislation and the revised Mineral Act make Community Development Agreements mandatory for mining development projects.

Well before the concept of CSR emerged, mining companies paid into community development funds. An early example was the Protectorate Mining Benefits Trust Fund in 1932. The Diamond Area Community Development Fund established in 2003 is a postcolonial equivalent. A percentage of revenue from the industry was to help pay for development projects in chiefdoms where mining was taking place (Govt. of Sierra Leone 1934; Ojukutu-Macauley and Keili 2008). Recent revisions in law call for contributions by companies to an agricultural development fund.

In the late 1980s, SRL implemented an Environmental and Community Development Programme (ECDP) for land reclamation and land rehabilitation. Rehabilitation efforts included aquaculture in mined-out

RACE, ETHNICITY, CLASS, AND GENDER IN MINING 105

dredge ponds, agriculture, reforestation of tailings areas, and construction of wells in villages. The Tegibeh Rice Co-operative was one of the initiatives under the program in 1988. The company supported farmers from three villages in rice cultivation. A total of 305 hectares (750 acres) would be cultivated over 4 years. Sixty hectares (150 acres) were cultivated in the first year. The arrangement was that the company would provide rice seeds, fertilizer, machinery, and infrastructure for threshing, drying, and storage. After harvest, the company would buy the rice at the same price as imported rice factoring in freight costs from the capital Freetown. Further, farmers could sell the rice elsewhere if it was more profitable. The only requirement was that participants in the program reimburse the cost of seeds and fertilizer. The project was considered a failure after one year because farmers only declared a portion of the rice harvest and did not repay the cost of seeds and fertilizer (personal Communication, DJY).

Rather than viewing the so-called failure as due to apathy on the part of farmers, it is important to understand the history and cultural context of rice, the staple in Sierra Leone. The inhabitants of the region within which the rutile lease lies have a long history of growing rice which was an export crop in the nineteenth century (Davidson 1969). Furthermore, the colonial government of The Colony would oftentimes fine chiefs in the Protectorate involved in conflicts with rice as currency. One example was when Acting Governor Samuel Rowe in the mid-1870s went to Imperi, Bagru, and Shenge to investigate unrest in Bumpe. He fined implicated chiefs 10,000 bushels of rice equivalent to 1,000 UK pounds sterling at the time (Fyfe 1962). Rice was still the main crop grown in the lease area based on a 1972 survey. As the area of mining operations expanded, more rice-growing areas were flooded and cassava overtook rice as the main crop (Labi 1972). Unlike rice, cassava is adaptable and can grow in various soils including low fertility types. Garri, a dry meal made from cassava, provides some revenue to local people. Some indigenous varieties of swamp rice can no longer be planted widely.

Anthropologist Paul Richards (1985/86) wrote about the cultural significance of rice and rice cultivation among the Mende ethnic group. For example, certain indigenous varieties are served to important guests, used in sacrifices to the ancestors and during special community ceremonies. In a 1942 survey of indigenous rice varieties grown by the Mende, 20 were identified as adapted to different land and water environments (Timberlake 1985). Also, introduced rice-growing schemes have an ugly colonial history of forced labor, fines, or imprisonment of farmers for not meeting quotas, the introduction of new varieties, and labor-intensive water control methods (Saylors 1967). So rice seeds imported from Louisiana, USA, and technical

106   CULTURE AND CONFLICTS IN SIERRA LEONE MINING

support were likely not acceptable incentive or compensation. Reciprocity, consultation, and consensus are at the core of indigenous communal life.

The wells in villages constructed in partnership with CARE were not always used. There is evidence of reforestation in some tailings areas. However, the fast-growing acacia tree species used are not indigenous and have little utility except for firewood. Cutting down trees for firewood defeats company efforts at rehabilitation.

Some early village resettlement efforts by SRL were poorly planned. Monetary compensation for property lost to mining did not result in the expected outcomes. Instead of rebuilding or investing in new crops, money was sometimes invested in other ventures. There was, therefore, not always visible evidence of the company's rehabilitation efforts. At a certain point, the company tried executing the entire relocation program. Yangatoke village was the first test case completed in 1990. Rather than paying money, SRL constructed houses, landscaped, planted economic trees, built wells, and supported agriculture. Interviews and focus group discussions conducted by a local NGO, the Organization for Research and Extension of Intermediate Technology (OREINT) partnering with Friends of the Earth, revealed that such efforts cannot replace the loss of culture and way of life and being part of a new mining economy has few tangible benefits for landlord indigenes. In protest of involuntary relocation communities oftentimes boycott facilities at new sites (Kamara 1997; Lamin et al. 1991).

More recent examples of CSR reported in the media include paying for school fees, supplies, and meals for hundreds of school children (*Awareness Times* 2011) and putting out a rapidly spreading fire in the main town near an iron ore mine. The Fire and Rescue Coordinator explained that the company had used over 5,000 liters of *its* water to extinguish the flames. A grateful resident was quoted as saying "We will continue to encourage them [the company] to assist us in such difficult times" (Samba 2012). The report on the fire rescue raises questions about the effectiveness of minerals-led sustainable development in host communities. First, where does government versus company responsibility lie in providing necessities such as water? Second, should poverty alleviation be part of a company's CSR? Third, to what extent do incidents like this reinforce antagonism over the loss of community control over natural resources?

Further, such gestures while magnanimous are not always well received by communities because of underlying grievances over powerful actors usurping their land and customary rights. This is a longtime and persistent concern in mining areas. Chiefs addressed the matter of the political, social, and economic inequities in the diamond areas in the 1957 petition to the Colonial Office in London mentioned earlier. They described the SLST

RACE, ETHNICITY, CLASS, AND GENDER IN MINING

"as the government in Kono because [it is] in control of almost everything" (*The London Times* 1957, 3). As such, the community's feeling is that companies operating on the ground should address their issues and problems.

Women, Children, and Mining

Women hold a variety of positions in the mining environment. They are Paramount Chiefs, license owners, miners, mine employees, entrepreneurs, traders, and household members. As Paramount Chiefs, custodians of lands on behalf of communities, they participate in negotiations with the government and companies and are entitled to 15 percent of surface rent paid by mining companies and other miscellaneous benefits. License holders listed in the 1935 Mines Department report included two women who were Creole strangers, Mrs. C. H. Macauley and Mrs. Annie R. McLeod (Govt. of Sierra Leone 1937). As haulers of water, collectors of ecological resources, and farmers, women are acutely aware of, and directly impacted by, changes to the landscape as discussed earlier. Women are caught up in the economic, environmental, and sociocultural changes caused by mining. They face the trauma of sexual abuse and violence (WoME 2021). The uncertainties around male miners achieving financial success and the conflicts between individualism and traditional communal responsibilities affect familial and gender relationships in households and community cohesion, more broadly (Rosen 1981).

In the traditional worldview, wealth accumulation by individuals, with no redistribution in communities, exposes them to charges of witchcraft. Fenton (1948, 16) documented that a wealthy man is said to possess snake medicine or Boa/Boman (*ndili* in the Mende language), which means "the 'medicine' of success." If he does not share this wealth, it becomes "a medicine that can injure his neighbors." Success or lack thereof by men in mining interpreted in traditional ways impacts gender dynamics. In a case study from Kono District, Rosen (1973) found that women also pay a price for acquiring wealth. There is a tremendous strain put on male–female relationships by economic opportunities, or lack thereof, created in the mining environment. Although there is a high failure rate among male miners, women are more successful in other businesses like petty and retail trade due to the large market from in-migrant populations. In frustration, men blame their circumstances on women. They exploit traditional controls to curtail the successes of women in their households by accusing them, for example, of using witchcraft to prevent their success. Nevertheless, women respond and are active in leading protests against injustices in the extraction environment. For example, as a last recourse, women withdraw to the protection of the *Sande* community

108   CULTURE AND CONFLICTS IN SIERRA LEONE MINING

events to protest openly and vent anger against male oppression without fear of repercussions. Outside the household, women in resettled villages in the African Minerals lease protested over poor access to water by blocking the railway line carrying ore to Pepel Port for shipment (Human Rights Watch 2014).

Ironically, water spirits that determine successful outcomes for male miners in the artisanal sector are typically female, like *Mami Wata*. Appropriate rituals are necessary to appease her (Jedrej 1974).

Women are typically gold and sometimes coltan miners. Recent studies show that while gold mining does provide income for women and their households, historical gender–social relations in traditional mining organizations constrain their participation and empowerment (Fofana-Ibrahim, Rutherford, and Buss 2020). Also, large-scale operations marginalize this livelihood. Women panned gold on streams flowing through hillslopes near their original villages to supplement household income in Tonkolili. This livelihood was lost when the company took over the hilltop for ancillary purposes. Hopefully, the Customary Lands Act 2022 with provisions on female empowerment in land use and rights will be implemented effectively. Under the law, committees assigned to managing communal lands and settling disputes should comprise 30 percent of women.

The government passed a gender empowerment Act in 2021. Further, the Mines and Minerals Development Act of 2021 incorporates policies and rules for the protection of women against violence and sexual exploitation, and other related issues in mining areas. Several civil society organizations are advocating for women in mining spaces. One such organization is Women on Mining and Extractives—Sierra Leone (WoME-SL) founded by a landlord-indigene lady from the Kono District. The organization brings awareness to the impacts of mining on women's lives, the lives of their children, and local communities. Efforts are supported by Development and Peace—CARITAS Canada. The Network for the Movement of Justice and Development (NMJD) partners with the global organization the Land for Life Movement to enlighten and empower women on issues like land rights, land grabs, food security, and conflicts.

Tied to women's challenges is the culturally problematic matter of child labor in artisanal mining as a subsistence livelihood to alleviate poverty in sub-Saharan African households. Sierra Leone ratified the ILO Convention on the Worst Forms of Child Labor (C182). Policies stemming from C182, and the International Program on the Elimination of Child Labor (IPEC), are based on Western perspectives of childhood and labor expectations. In the traditional context, where children cannot access Western education in schools, they learn skills that help contribute to household income and

RACE, ETHNICITY, CLASS, AND GENDER IN MINING 109

make them productive members of their communities. Farming, fishing, and artisanal mining are examples of customary economic livelihoods.

Women and children have long participated in Sierra Leone mining as implied by the Minerals Ordinance of 1927. The Governor could make rules "restricting or prohibiting the employment of women and children in prospecting or mining operations." Child miners are called "half shovels" because they can only do light digging and typically mine in family groups. There are allegations of abuse of child labor by foreign companies in media reports. Children sometimes willingly participate to earn money to support their families and pay for a Western education for themselves. Children attending school often join their mothers at mine sites after school (Govt. of Sierra Leone 2018b; Maconachie and Hilson 2016; Sierra Leone Web 2023). The government has made strides in making Western education more accessible through the New Direction agenda. Until easily accessible, affordable, and quality Western education becomes widespread, children will continue to participate in subsistence livelihoods that support households and teach them skills and responsibility.

Chapter 7

BETWEEN A ROCK AND
A HARD PLACE

Malfunctions endemic in the existing land rights administration cannot be permanently addressed unless the system as presently established is dismantled and re-engineered. This exercise must recognize the empirical realities associated with operating parallel systems of land rights administration; comprising customary institutions as part and parcel of the social and political organization of territorial groups, and formal systems governed by statutory law. (Govt of Sierra Leone 2015c, 70).

The stories of turmoil discussed here reflect the convoluted and culturally complex relationships developed over the years among landlord-indigene communities, strangers including companies, and the state in mining spaces. Caught between a rock and a hard place are chiefs as traditional governance leaders and government officials of a peripheral country. In colonial history, chiefs are largely accused of oppression, authoritarianism, terrorism, slave trading, and sustaining a gerontocracy that exploits and marginalizes youth. These behaviors were justification to establish a Protectorate under the supervision of Great Britain according to District Commissioner Thomas Alldridge who signed several treaties with chiefs. The creation of the Frontier Police Force in 1893 to enforce this policy was no less ruthless. The force was so feared that locals sometimes abandoned their farms and hid in the forests to escape the intimidation and brutality. The subsequent Protectorate Ordinance established state dominance over the chieftaincy governance which has been in place since. Chiefs govern within the framework of the state and in many ways are caught between their traditional roles and the state's expectations of their leadership (Abraham 2003; Alldridge 1910; Conteh 2013; Fyfe 1962; Peters 2011).

Specific to development projects, chiefs are caught between the forces of tradition and modernity. They both benefit from and object to the actions of development projects like mining. Chiefs frequently protest and petition the national government as we have seen in earlier examples discussed

112   CULTURE AND CONFLICTS IN SIERRA LEONE MINING

(Akiwumi 2018). Nevertheless, discord arises between them and their subjects, particularly young people who see chiefs as complicit in projects. A farmer impacted by a large land development project summarized the view of chiefs as a party to long-term leases from a landlord-indigenes perspective:

> If a chief sells the land which belongs to a village and people are residing in that village, can he still boast of being the chief? No! The person who bought the land should now be the chief because he is the landowner. So you who are selling your land should no longer say that you are chiefs. You are only strangers. (Welthungerhilfe-SLE, 2012, 30)

To compound this sentiment, chiefs of resettled villages oftentimes do not command the same respect from their subjects at the new site (personal communication with WOME Director 2023).

Another matter of concern for landlord-indigenes in mining areas is that sometimes their chiefs allow strangers to hold leadership positions as councilors on the Chiefdom Councils. The belief is that such individuals from other ethnic groups are not deeply rooted in the land and therefore do not have the passion or commitment to fight fervently for community rights. An illustration of this concern is when the co-chair of The Land Owners Federation claimed that a stranger supported by some Chiefdom Councilors was behind some unrest in Lower Banta Chiefdom in the rutile mining area in 1986. Using the customary expression for fomenting trouble, he alleged that the stranger's intention was "to wage war on the people of Banta" (Sierra Rutile Ltd. 2003a).

In reality, some landlord-indigenes may not fully understand the limitations put on their chiefs by the state's development agenda and laws where they cannot be effective custodians of the land in traditional ways. There is a historical precedence to the position of chiefs vis-a-vis strangers established in the nineteenth-century trade in timber and other land resources. Chiefs compromised or were coerced because of new wealth from forest exploitation, domineering entrepreneurial strangers and pressures of the British colonial government to cede territory. Strangers were problematic within landlord-indigene communities in the region now covered by the SRL lease. The region was loosely divided up into "country" rather than district. For example, Warrior Karboka was more powerful than his landlord Thomas Caulker of Bagru Country. Warrior-chief Gbanyah governed from Senehun even though the Caulkers were the landlords in Bumpe Country. Sometimes chiefs succumbing to British sovereignty was the lesser of the two evils compared to the hegemony of stranger entrepreneurs and warriors (Fyfe 1962).

BETWEEN A ROCK AND A HARD PLACE   113

In 1882, Chief Betsy Gay of the Jong Country requested British protection from stranger chiefs such as Cleveland, Farmah, and Lady (Lahai) Serrifoo who were planning to wage war against her and the people of the Jong country. Her supporters, some of whom were strangers, appealed to then Governor Havelock on her behalf extolling "Miss Betsy Gay, the daughter of the late Marrigba ... the right owner of the soil." Chief Gay's troubles, they said, were caused by

> strangers who have come from different parts of the country and settled here, notably Lahsurru, a Foulah man, who worked his way down to this river with war and who is no trader but always is ready to prepare war. (Sierra Leone Government Papers 1882, 10)

In Imperi Country, Chiefs Ka Tegbe of Gendama, Ba Shia of Bogo, and Gbana Bunje of Gangama strongly protested to the colonial government about the domineering influence of wealthy Creole entrepreneur Solomon Augustus Benjamin Macfoy, the self-titled Sherbro Monarch. Christopher Fyfe (1962, 508) in *A History of Sierra Leone* described him as "a man feared rather than loved, alarming even to those who admired him." Anecdotal stories tell that his nickname among Creoles in The Colony was Abuke Macfoy. Abuke is the Yoruba word for a hunchback. His trade partner in Britain was the Manchester firm of Callender, Sykes, and Mather who had connections in the Colonial Office in London. With their help, Macfoy was able to bypass colonial administrators in Sierra Leone and influence policy on additional lands to be brought under British control to support his business ventures. To curb the powerful influence of such an individual stranger, the colonial government passed the Concessions Ordinance of 1924 so that chiefs could invite other competitors to conduct business in their territories (Fyfe 1962).

Since the seminal work for UNESCO by the late Sierra Leonean historian and anthropologist Arthur Abraham in 1978 titled *Cultural Policy in Sierra Leone*, the government has tried to incorporate more cultural awareness and sensitivity in policies and laws (Abraham 1978). Although national governance still supersedes customary rule there is some progress towards more equitable reforms. The Constitution of Sierra Leone of 1991 which is undergoing a Constitutional Review Process supports "traditional Sierra Leonean institutions compatible with national development." The document also states that "The institution of chieftaincy as established by customary law and usage and its non-abolition by legislation is hereby guaranteed and preserved" (Govt. of Sierra Leone 1991). The preceding constitution of 1978 declared that customary law and usage be respected and

114 CULTURE AND CONFLICTS IN SIERRA LEONE MINING

that community interest be central to the development, use and conservation of natural resources (Govt. of Sierra Leone 1978).

National government officials including the president frequently reiterate their support of the chieftaincy institution. There have been several recent regulatory reforms to strengthen traditional governance institutions while keeping a measure of state control. Some current examples are the Chiefs of Sierra Leone: Code of Ethics in 2014, the Chiefdom and Traditional Administration Policy in 2012, the Chieftaincy Act 2009, and the Local Government Act 2004. The document "Chiefs of Sierra Leone Code of Ethics and Service Standards" is a collaboration between the National Council of Paramount Chiefs and the Ministry of Local Government and Rural Development supported by DFID. It provides guidelines for the "acceptable standards of service, behaviour and integrity required of Paramount Chiefs, Section Chiefs, Village and Town Chiefs in the dispensation of their authority" (Awoko Publications 2014b). Overall, Paramount Chiefs are to preserve and promote culture as appropriate, be custodians of customs but move toward modernity, and help implement the government's development agenda. They must cease practices such as forced labor and coercion of subjects linked to a heritage of war, conquest, and iron fist rule. The government's commitment is to continue to strengthen the capacity of paramount chiefs to transform their communities and the lives of their people. Symbolic actions by the government to enhance the prestige and dignity of chiefs included the presentation of the staff of office and a Durbar of Chiefs in April 2011. The ceremony was last held at Sierra Leone's Independence in 1961 (A Z Media Corp 2023; Govt. of Sierra Leone 2009b, 2014b, 2015d; Sierra Express Media 2011; Sierraloaded 2022; UNDP 2012).

The national government is in a hard place of its own leading a peripheral nation state with a colonial legacy. Its mandate is to generate the revenues needed for modern development. With a development agenda largely based on mineral extraction revenue, pressure from global markets, and geographical expansion by companies in search of minerals, there are challenges to protecting cultural heritage. Much of the country is covered in exploration and mine leases so that continuing land conflicts are inevitable. The development agenda caught up in the structural constraints of a global economic system disadvantages the traditional land use system and landlord–stranger governance. The NLP 2015 acknowledged the reality of a dual governance system as quoted above. The new land laws of 2022 are an effort at "dismantling and engineering," but how these changes might impact the mining sector is unclear at this time.

Chapter 8

CONCLUSION

My goal in this book was to explore cultural dynamics (cultural alienation, cultural hybridity, cultural resistance, and cultural evolution) embedded in a world system commodity chain. I devised a conceptual model combining premises from world systems and postcolonial theories and the landlord–stranger paradigm to analyze and better understand the cultural differences in mining that are a root cause of persistent low-intensity conflicts in extraction areas.

I posed some important guiding questions to support my premise of a culturally unequal exchange: To recap: How does the Sierra Leone government address the cultural differences in land management embedded in mineral commodity chains in policy and law? Is there an asymmetric transfer of cultural resources and norms from core and semi-peripheral countries to peripheral nations? Can this transfer be conceptualized as a culturally unequal exchange? Is "illicit" artisanal mining a form of cultural resistance against the impacts of incorporation on customary land rights? Do cultural resistance and cultural hybridity in Sierra Leone mining areas pose challenges to effective incorporation through mineral commodity chains? Can cultural resistance in the Sierra Leone mining sector trigger a development evolution that moves beyond capitalist extractivism toward new development trajectories that embody African cultural values? Or will the continuing marginalization of African cultural perspectives persist in the face of a capitalist global economy inexorably driving toward cultural universalism?

Operating within the commodity chain are Western cultural concepts of mining governed by state laws and indigenous artisanal mining as a time-honored subsistence livelihood managed by the landlord–stranger institution and power associations. The latter is seen as poorly managed and illicit, a colonial legacy, and the former as legal and economically efficient. The cultural differences and power imbalance in this arrangement have generated low-intensity and persistent conflict situations integral to the mining industry in Sierra Leone since its inception.

116   CULTURE AND CONFLICTS IN SIERRA LEONE MINING

The state faces legislative and policy dilemmas, a colonial legacy, in trying to reconcile customary land management—the landlord–stranger relationship—with Western notions of mining land use. There have been rapid changes in policies and laws to facilitate mineral extraction amid cultural conflicts. Mining multinationals are privileged and powerful strangers through state laws. Although laws recognize them as nonnatives or strangers paying annual surface rent, they are not subject to other tenets of the landlord–stranger relationship concerning land use and rights. The mine spawns a new social hierarchy in landlord-indigene host communities. The multinational as an influential stranger employs other strangers of varied race, ethnicity, and nationality. Caucasian mine employees historically dominate top management positions in mining companies and racial discrimination against Africans is a real or perceived issue. Some violate the customary etiquette and norms of host communities. The entrenchment of various categories of strangers in mining areas exacerbates historic struggles over autochthony and citizenship, class, and gender oppression.

Introduced into the environment are symbols of a different culture—massive dredges looming in the landscape, earth-moving bulldozers and excavators that obliterate the natural and human landscape, hazardous chemicals used in mineral processing, road networks for trucks and other vehicles, and elite modern fenced mine camps amid indigenous communities. Tailings ponds and stockpiles dot the landscape. In contrast, the landlord-indigene cultural perspective of land use is rooted in deep spiritual connections to lands settled by ancestors including sacred places and burial grounds, and the right to access resources or livelihoods on those lands including from externally generated mining. Further, there is a weak understanding of compulsory land acquisition with the loss of traditional livelihoods. So political promises by the state and company CSR, and CDAs are rarely considered adequate compensation.

Landlord-indigene communities interpret and make sense of environmental and sociocultural changes within their worldview and protest the loss of ecological resources and livelihoods and pollution of water sources. Mining projects erase places significant to customary life and livelihoods. Legislation since the colonial period has confined artisanal miners to the periphery of large company leases or away from leases altogether. Leases oftentimes coincide with historic customary mining areas. The economic transformation of households from mining alienates women and weakens their traditional community and household influences. Along the lines of economic unequal exchange and ecological unequal exchange in world system chain processes the above descriptors represent "cultural unequal exchange," an asymmetric transfer of Western cultural resources and norms associated with mineral exploitation.

CONCLUSION   117

As such, illicit mining becomes a form of cultural resistance to underscore ancestral rights to land, livelihoods, and life in general. Territorial claims to lands, rights to resources based on indigeneity, power associations, sacred places, indigenous knowledge, and conceptions of the environment are fundamental to the sustainability of customary life and cultural heritage. Cultural, socioeconomic, and environmental sustainability are inextricably linked. Unfortunately, illicit mining and smuggling as resistance also have consequences for the environment and cultural sustainability. For instance, the increasing use of hazardous chemicals like mercury and inefficient pseudo-modern technologies contaminate soils and water and pollute the air. This protest right to artisanal mining and smuggling as livelihood does threaten the flow of mineral commodity chains and the generation of much-needed revenue for the nation's development.

In the struggle to preserve cultural heritage, landlord-indigene households support and organize antisystemic protests against loss and continual threats to a way of life. Periodic outbursts of violence and damage to company property compromise incorporation. Cultural hybridity also compromises incorporation as there is allegiance to historic mining organizations, in part. In diamond mining areas, the customary stranger became the "statutory alien" and the Jula gold mining financier, the supporter. Both customary and introduced modes of mining operate concurrently in a competitive environment. Another example is the contradiction of child labor at mines prohibited by state law but children participating in a customary subsistence livelihood to help alleviate household poverty. Cultural disruption and cultural hybridity caused by mining activities force some forms of cultural evolution. For example, communities adapt to alternative livelihood possibilities in a deteriorated landscape or adopt the use of deleterious imported chemicals in the hope of increasing output.

Although cultural resistance and antisystemic protests by households threaten the smooth flow of mineral commodity chains, global expansion for important minerals affects the country. External pressure from global markets, a national government needing revenue, traditional governance and ethnic struggles for survival and opportunity, and individual political agendas are factors at play. The Sierra Leone government has crafted new land laws and reformed some mining laws. However, a careful examination of some laws reveals inequitable colonial-era clauses still securely embedded. The laws align with African regional development instruments and the global mining agenda (e.g., AMV, EITI, and ICMM) that reference cultural inclusivity, among other things, like gender equity. Whether the changes effectively embody African cultural values that the majority of Sierra Leoneans can relate to is debatable.

118   CULTURE AND CONFLICTS IN SIERRA LEONE MINING

The government's efforts to effectively address culturally sensitive considerations in mining policy and law remain a challenge. Because of the power imbalances in the dual governance system and the Sierra Leone's weak position in the global hierarchy of nations, we see the continual erosion of indigenous knowledge and perspectives on mining, land use, and rights. A tumultuous march toward cultural universalism is ongoing.

REFERENCES

Abdullah I. (ed.). 2004. *Between Democracy and Terror: The Sierra Leone Civil War.* Dakar: CODESRIA.

Abraham, A. 2003. *An Introduction to the Pre-colonial History of the Mende of Sierra Leone.* Lewiston, NY: The Edwin Mellen Press.

Abraham, A. 1978. *Cultural Policy in Sierra Leone.* Studies and Documents in Cultural Policies. Paris, France: UNESCO.

Abraham, A., and Gaima, E. A. R. 1996. Ethnographic survey of the Kalantuba Limba of Kalansagoia Chiefdom, Tonkolili District, Northern Province, Sierra Leone. Institute of African Studies. *Occasional Paper No. 5,* Fourah Bay College, University of Sierra Leone.

African Business. 2019. "Sierra Leone's Diamond Industry Must Be Reformed: Smuggling and Corruption Leads to Tens of Millions of Dollars of Potential Tax Revenue Being Lost Each Year." https://african.business/2019/05/economy/sierra-leones-diamond-industry/.

African Union (AU). 2016a. "OAU/AU Treaties, Conventions, Protocols & Charters." http://www.au.int/en/treaties.

African Union (AU). 2016b. "Agenda 2063." http://www.au.int/en/agenda2063.

African Union (AU). 2010. "Framework and Guidelines on Land Policy in Africa. Land Policy in Africa: A Framework to Strengthen Land Rights, Enhance Productivity and Secure Livelihoods." UC-ECA-AfDB Consortium, Addis Ababa, Ethiopia. http://www.uneca.org/sites/default/files/PublicationFiles/fg_on_land_policy_eng.pdf.

Africa Young Voices (AYV), 2013. Illegal mining on increase in Bombali. By E.L.L. Sannoh, AYV Newspaper online, August 2 2013. http://africayoungvoices.com/2013/08/illegal-mining-on-increase-in-bombali/.

Ahluwalia, P. 2012. *Politics and Post-colonial Theory: African Inflections.* London: Routledge.

Akam, S. 2010. "After diamonds, iron ore foments Sierra Leone tensions." Reuters. December 8, 2010. https://www.reuters.com/article/uk-sierraleone-resources/after-diamonds-iron-foments-sierra-leone-tensions-idUKTRE6B73A020101208.

Akiwumi, F. A. 2018. "Cultural Conundrums in African Land Governance: Agribusiness in Sierra Leone." *Geography Research Forum* 37: 37–60. https://grf.bgu.ac.il/index.php/GRF/article/view/532.

Akiwumi, F. A. 2014. "Strangers and Sierra Leone Mining: Cultural Heritage and Sustainable Development Challenges." *Journal of Cleaner Production* 84: 773–782. https://doi.org/10.1016/j.jclepro.2013.12.078.

Akiwumi, F. A. 2012. "Global Incorporation and Local Conflict: Sierra Leonean Mining Regions." *Antipode* 44 (3): 581–600. https://doi.org/10.1111/j.1467-8330.2011.00945.x.

120   CULTURE AND CONFLICTS IN SIERRA LEONE MINING

Akiwumi, F. A. 2008a. "An Assessment of Hazards from Gold Mining in Sierra Leone." *Papers of the Applied Geography Conference* 31: 10–18.

Akiwumi, F. A., and D. R. Butler. 2008b. "Mining and Environmental Change in Sierra Leone, West Africa: A Remote Sensing and Hydrogeomorphological Study." *Environmental Monitoring and Assessment* 142: 309–318. https://doi.org/10.1007/s10661-007-9930-9.

Akiwumi, F. A. 2006. Environmental and Social Change in Southwestern Sierra Leone: Timber Extraction (1832–1898) and Rutile Mining (1967–2005). Ph.D. dissertation Texas State University – San Marcos.

Akiwumi, F. A., Lamin, Ahmed S., Conteh, Mohamed, Leopold, Reginald, and Ibrahim, Babatunde B. 1990. "Water management and environmental impact assessment of the Sierra Rutile mining operations." Report to Sierra Rutile Ltd., Freetown, Sierra Leone: Environmental and Scientific Consulting Group (ESCG).

Akiwumi, F. A. 1987. "The appraisal of water supply potential at the new locations for Pejebu, Vaama and Mondoko." Report to Sierra Rutile, Ltd. Freetown, Sierra Leone.

Alldridge, Thomas J. 1910. *A Transformed Colony: Sierra Leone as It was and as It Is, Its Progress, Peoples, Native Customs and Undeveloped Wealth.* London: Seeley and Co. Ltd.

Amanor, Kojo S. 2010. "Family Values, Land Sales and Agricultural Commodification in Southeastern Ghana." *Africa* 80 no. 1: 104–125. https://doi.org/10.3366/E0001972009001284.

Amnesty International. 2022. "Sierra Leone: No Diamond Is Worth the Life of a Community." https://www.amnesty.org/en/latest/news/2022/12/sierra-leone-aucun-diamant-ne-vaut-la-vie-dune-communaute/.

Atherton, J. H. 1980. Speculations on Functions of Some Prehistoric Archaeological Materials from Sierra Leone. In *West African Culture Dynamics: Archaeological and Historical Perspectives*, edited by B. K. Swartz, and R. E. Dumett, 259–278. Great Britain: Mouton Publishers.

Atherton, J. H. 1972. "Excavations at Kamabai and Yagala Rock Shelters." *West African Journal of Archaeology*, 2: 259–278.

Awareness Times. 2009. "NaCSA & Hope-SL Symbolic Reparation in Jawei, Daru, Kailahun." Nov 9, 2009. http://www.news.sl/drwebsite/publish/article_200513593.shtml.

Awoko Publications. 2014b. "Sierra Leone News: Illicit mining pervades GRNP. By S. B. Moriba." May 7, 2014. http://awoko.org/2014/05/07/sierra-leone-news-illicit-mining-pervades-grnp/.

Awoko Publications. 2014d. "Sierra Leone News: Ethics guide for PCs launched in Bo." https://awokonewspaper.sl/sierra-leone-news-ethics-guide-for-pcs-launched-in-bo/.

Awoko Publications. 2010a. "We are dying because of iron ore – Kemedugu people cry." https://awokonewspaper.sl/we-are-dying-because-of-iron-ore-kemedugu-people-cry/

Awoko Publications. 2010b. "Lunsar strike has nothing to do with LMC – David Keili." http://awoko.org/2010/08/12/lunsar-strike-has-nothing-to-do-with-lmc-david-keili/.

Awoko Publications. 2010c. "Lunsar strike has nothing to do with LMC—David Keili." http://awoko.org/2010/08/12/lunsar-strike-has-nothing-to-do-with-lmc-david-keili/.

A-Z Multimedia Corp. 2023. "President Bio Gives Staff of Authority to 10 Elected Paramount Chiefs in Northern Region." https://a-zsl.com/president-bio-gives-staff-of-authority-to-10-elected-paramount-chiefs-in-northern-region/.

Bair, J. 2009. *Frontiers of Commodity Chain Research.* Stanford, CA: Stanford University Press.

REFERENCES

121

Bair, J. 2005. "Global Capitalism and Commodity Chains: Looking Back, Going Forward." *Competition and Change* 9(2): 153–180. https://doi.org/10.1179/102452905X45382.

Baker, H. A., Diawara, M., and Lindeborg, R. H. (Eds.). 1996. *Black British Cultural Studies: A Reader.* Chicago: University of Chicago Press.

Basu, P. 2013. "Memoryscapes and Multi-Sited Methods: Researching Cultural Memory in Sierra Leone." In *Research Methods for Memory Studies*, edited by E. Keightley, and M. Pickering, 115–131. Edinburgh: Edinburgh University Press.

Bigart, H. 1960. "Calmness rules in Sierra Leone: Colony prepares for stable independence—plans to stay in Commonwealth." Special to the *New York Times*, March 27, 1960.

Black, E. 2022. "Sierra Leone lawsuit against diamond mine runs up against corporate opacity." 17 February 2022. https://news.mongabay.com/2022/02/sierra-leone-lawsuit-against-diamond-mine-runs-up-against-corporate-opacity/.

Blyden III, E. W. 1959. "Sierra Leone: The pattern of constitutional change." Ph.D. diss., Harvard University.

Bøås, M. 2014. *The Politics of Conflict Economies: Miners, Merchants and Warriors in the African Borderland.* New York: Routledge.

Boatcă, M., Komlosy, A., and Hans-Heinrich, N. 2017. *Global Inequalities in World System Perspective: Theoretical Debates and Methodological Innovations.* Boca Raton, FL: CRC Press.

Boone, S. A. 1986. *Radiance from the Waters: Ideals of Feminine Beauty in Mende Art.* New Haven, CT: Yale University Press.

Boskoff, A. 1969. *Theory in American Sociology: Major Sources and Applications.* New York: Crowell.

Briggs, J., and Sharp, J. 2004. Indigenous Knowledges and Development: A Postcolonial Caution. *Third World Quarterly* 25(4): 661–676.

Brima, A. 2021. "Chinese Mining Company Accused of 'ruining' Sierra Leone Village." *Mail and Guardian.* 23 July 2021. https://mg.co.za/africa/2021-07-23-chinese-mining-company-accused-of-ruining-sierra-leone-village/.

Brooks, G. E. 2003. *Eurafricans in Western Africa: Commerce, Social Status, Gender, and Religious Observance from the Sixteenth to Eighteenth Century.* Athens, OH: Ohio University Press.

Brooks, G. E., and Beauregard, E. E. 1993. *Landlords and Strangers: Ecology, Society and Trade in Western Africa, 1000–1630.* Boulder, CO: Westview Press.

Bunker, S. G. 2019. "Toward a Theory of Ecologically Unequal Exchange." In *Ecologically Unequal Exchange*, edited by R. Frey, P. Gellert, and H. Dahms, 13–47. London: Palgrave Macmillan.

Burchardt, H. J., and Dietz, K. 2014. "(Neo-) Extractivism–A New Challenge for Development Theory from Latin America." *Third World Quarterly* 35(3): 468–486. https://doi.org/10.1080/01436597.2014.893488.

Canós-Donnay, S. 2019. "The Empire of Mali." African History: Oxford Research Encyclopedia of African History. https://doi.org/10.1093/acrefore/9780190277734.013.266.

CARITAS Canada. 2018. "Development and Peace: The negative impacts of mining on women in Sierra Leone." https://www.devp.org/en/legacy/negative-benefits-mining-women-sierra-leone/.

Cartier, L., and Burge, M. 2011. "Agriculture and Artisanal Gold Mining in Sierra Leone: Alternatives or Complements." *Journal of International Development* 23(8): 1080–1099. https://doi.org/10.1002/jid.1833.

CEMMATS. 2021. "Assessment of the Impact of EITI and Socioeconomic Benefits Derived from Subnational Extractive Revenues by Mining Communities. Ministry of Mines and Mineral Resources Extractive Industries Technical Assistance Project—Phase 2, Final Report" September 2021.

Chanock, M. 2006. "Customary Law, Sustainable Development and the Failing State." In *The Role of Customary Law in Sustainable Development*, edited by P. Orebech, F. Bosselman, J. Bjarup, D. Callies, M. Chanock, and H. Petersen, 338–383. Cambridge: Cambridge University Press.

Chase-Dunn, C. 2018. *Rise and Demise: Comparing World Systems*. New York: Routledge.

Clark, J. I. 1966. *Sierra Leone in Maps*. London: University of London Press Ltd.

Claus R. J., and Padgett B. H. et al. 1972. "Report on the Phase 1 Exploration Program S.E.P.L. No. 2095 Southern Province, Sierra Leone, West Africa." Sierra Rutile Ltd. Geological Reports.

Cleeve, E. E. 1997. *Multinational Enterprises in Development: The Mining Industry of Sierra Leone*. Vermont: Ashgate Publishing Co.

Colonial Office. 1958. "Sierra Leone Report 1956." Freetown: H. M. Stationery Office, 73.

Colonial Office. 1949. "Annual Report on Sierra Leone for the Year 1947." London: H. M. Stationery Office.

Colonial Office. 1947. "Annual Report on Sierra Leone for the Year 1946." London: H. M. Stationery Office, 29–30. IPS

Conteh, M. N. 2013. "The Institution of Paramount Chieftaincy in Sierra Leone An Introduction to its History and Electoral Process." https://necsl.org/files/pdf/media/the%20institution%20of%20paramount%20chieftaincy%20in%20sierra%20leone.pdf.

Conteh, P. S. 2009. "Fundamental Concepts of Limba Traditional Religion and its Effects on Limba Christianity and Vice Versa in Sierra Leone in the Past Three Decades." Ph.D. diss., University of South Africa.

Conteh, J. S. 1979. "Diamond Mining and Kono Religious Institutions: A Study in Social Change." Ph.D. diss., University of Indiana.

Cormier-Salem, M., and Bassett, T. J. 2007. "Introduction: Nature as Local Heritage in Africa Longstanding Concerns, New Challenges." *Africa* 77(1):1–14. 10.3366/afr.2007.77.1.1.

Coser, L. A. 1972. "The Alien as a Servant of Power: Court Jews and Christian Renegades." *American Sociological Review* 37(5): 574–581. https://doi.org/10.2307/2093452.

Cronje, F., and Chenga, C. S. 2009. "Sustainable Social Development in the South African Mining Sector." *Development Southern Africa* 26(3): 413–427. https://doi.org/10.1080/03768350903086788.

D'Angelo, L. 2022. "Operation Parasite: Diamonds, Smallpox, and Mass Expulsions of Strangers in Colonial Sierra Leone." *Canadian Journal of African Studies / Revue canadienne des études africaines* 57(1) (2023): 139–159. DOI: 10.1080/00083968.2022.2033629.

D'Angelo, L. 2019. Changing Environments, Occult Protests and Social Memories in Sierra Leone. In *The Omnipresent Past. Historical Anthropology of Africa and African Diaspora*, edited by D. M. Bondarenko, and M. L. Butovskaya, 46–65. Moscow: LRC Publishing House.

D'Angelo, L. 2018. From Traces to Carpets Unravelling Labour Practices in the Mines of Sierra Leone. In *Micro-Spatial Histories of Global Labour*, edited by C. De Vito,

REFERENCES
123

and A. Gerritsen, 313–342. London: Palgrave Macmillan, Cham. https://doi.org/10.1007/978-3-319-58490-4_12.

D'Angelo, L. 2014. "Who Owns the Diamonds? The Occult Economy of Diamond Mining in Sierra Leone." *Africa* 84(02): 269–293. https://doi.org/10.1017/S0001972013000752.

Daily Mail. 1956a. "LegCo Passes Bill to Eject 'Strangers'. Dunbar Warns Against Armed Resistance." *The Daily Mail (Freetown)*, 26 October 1956.

Daily Mail. 1956b. "Governor's Guiding Hand." *The Daily Mail (Freetown)*, 22 October 1956.

Daily Mail. 1956c. "Strangers Are Crowding Us Out. Paul Dunbar Tells of Kono Problem." *The Daily Mail (Freetown)*, 22 October 1956.

Daily Mail. 1954. "'Stranger' Clause." *The Daily Mail (Freetown)*, 18 March 1954.

Davidson, J. 1969. Trade and politics in the Sherbro hinterland. Ph.D. dissertation, University of Wisconsin.

Doortmont, M. R. 2005. *The Pen-Pictures of Modern Africans and African Celebrities by Charles Francis Hutchison: A Collective Biography of Elite Society in the Gold Coast Colony.* Leiden: Brill.

Dorjahn, V. R., and Fyfe, C. 1962. "Landlord and Stranger: Change in Tenancy Relations in Sierra Leone." *Journal of African History* 3: 391–397. https://doi.org/10.1017/S0021853700003315.

Dorman, S., Hammett, D., and Nugent, S. (eds.). 2007. *Making Nations, Creating Strangers: States and Citizenship in Africa.* Leiden, The Netherlands: Brill N.V.

Downey, L., Bonds, E., and Clark, K. 2010. "Natural Resource Extraction, Armed Violence, and Environmental Degradation." *Organization and Environment* 23: 417–445. https://doi.org/10.1177/108602661038590.

Dummett, R. E. 1998. *El Dorado in West Africa: The Gold-mining Frontier, African Labor, and Colonial Capitalism in the Gold Coast, 1875–1900.* Athens, OH: The Ohio University Press.

Dunaway, W. A. 2014. "Bringing Commodity Chain Analysis Back to Its World Systems Roots: Rediscovering Women's Work and Households." *Journal of World-Systems Research* 20(1): 64–81. https://doi.org/10.5195/jwsr.2014.576.

Dunaway, W. A. 2010. "Nonwaged Peasants in the Modern World System: African Households as Dialectical Units of Capitalist Exploitation and Indigenous Resistance, 1890–1930." *The Journal of Philosophical Economics* 4(1): 19–57. https://doi.org/10.46298/jpe.10604.

Dunaway, W. A. 2003. "Ethnic Conflict in the Modern World System: The Dialectics of Counter-Hegemonic Resistance in an Age of Transition." *Journal of World-Systems Research* 9(1): 3–34. https://doi.org/10.5195/jwsr.2003.258.

Dunaway, W. A. 2001. "The Double Register of History: Situating the Forgotten Woman and Her Household in Capitalist Commodity Chains." *Journal of World-Systems Research* 7(1): 2–29. https://doi.org/10.5195/jwsr.2001.182.

Dunham, K. 1983. "Biographical Memoirs of Fellows of the Royal Society." Vol 29, Nov 1983: 158–176 (Frank Dixey. 7 April 1892–1 November 1982).

Edozie, R. K., and Gottschalk, K. 2014. *The African Union's Africa: New Pan-African Initiatives in Global Governance.* Michigan: MSU Press.

EITI. 2021. "Sierra Leone 2019" EITI report. https://eiti.org/countries/sierra-leone.

Elliot, I. L. 1966. "Dispersion of arsenic and molybdenum in surface drainage, Sierra Leone." Ph.D. diss., University of London.

124   CULTURE AND CONFLICTS IN SIERRA LEONE MINING

Embassy of the People's Republic of China (PRC). 2018. "The Administrations for Gold Mining in Sierra Leone Embassy of the People's Republic of China in the Republic of Sierra Leone." 2018-07-29 01:19. http://sl.china-embassy.gov.cn/eng/sgxx/201807/t20180729_5981795.htm.

Falconer, C. A. 2019. "'No to Mining Yes to Life': An Ethnographic Account of Buen Vivir in Postneoliberal Ecuador" Ph.D. diss., University of Toronto.

Fallah-Williams, J. 2021a. "Sierra Leone: Minister of mines accused of issuing illegal and unlawful licences to Chinese companies." *Sierra Leone Telegraph* 15 Jul 2021 https://www.business-humanrights.org/en/latest-news/sierra-leone-minister-of-mines-accused-of-issuing-illegal-and-unlawful-licences-to-chinese-companies/.

Fallah-Williams, J. 2021b. "Sierra Leone: Communities complain about a mysterious 'new' illnesses in women and children as illegal mining is uncovered." Sierra Leone Telegraph 24 Jun 2021. Business and Human Rights Resource Centre. https://www.business-humanrights.org/en/latest-news/sierra-leone-communities-complain-about-a-mysterious-new-illnesses-in-women-and-children-as-illegal-mining-is-uncovered/.

Falola, T. 1985. "From Hospitality to Hostility: Ibadan and Strangers, 1830–1904." *Journal of African History* 26: 51–68. https://doi.org/10.1017/S0021853700023082.

Fanthorpe R. and Maconachie R. 2010. "Beyond the 'Crisis of Youth'? Mining, Farming, and Civil Society in Post-war Sierra Leone." *African Affairs* 109(435):251–272.

Fanthorpe, R. 2007. "Sierra Leone: The Influence of the Secret Societies with Special Reference to Female Genital Mutilation." Writenet Report to. United Nations High Commissioner for Refugees, Status Determination and Protection Information Section (DIPS).

Fanthorpe, R. 2001. "Neither Citizen nor Subject? Lumpen Agency and the Legacy of Native Administration in Sierra Leone." *African Affairs* 100(400): 363–386.

FBIS. 1982. "Illegal strangers warned to quit mining areas." *Foreign Broadcast International Service*: Subsaharan Africa Report No. 2669. JPRS 81437, 3 August 1982, Springfield VA 22161.

Fenton, J. S. 1948. *Outline of Native Law in Sierra Leone.* Freetown, SL: Government Printer.

Ferme, M. 2000. *The Underneath of Things: Violence and the Everyday in Sierra Leone.* Berkeley, CA: Berkeley University Press.

FESS. 2007. "Natural Resources and Conflict. Mining and Minerals: Tiffany & Co. Foundation sponsored project." https://www.fess-global.org/tiffany.cfm.

Fofana, L. 1998a. "Sierra Leone Stops Foreign Mining." *Electronic Mail and Guardian.* Johannesburg, South Africa, March 31, 1998. www.mg.co.za/mg/news/98mar2/31mar-slmining.

Fofana, L. 1998b. "Economy of Sierra Leone: Taking Back the Mines." *Inter Press Service NEXIS.* 30 March 1998. http://www.ipsnews.net/1998/03/economysierra-leone-taking-back-the-mines/.

Fowler-Lunn, K. 1938. *The Gold Missus: A Woman Prospector in Sierra Leone.* New York: W. W. Norton.

Frank, B. 1995. "Permitted and Prohibited Wealth: Commodity-Possessing Spirits, Economic Morals, and the Goddess Mami Wata in West Africa." *Ethnology* 34(4): 331–346. https://doi.org/10.2307/3773945.

Freudenberger, M. S., Carney, J. A., and Lebbie, A. R. 1997. "Resiliency and Change in Common Property Regimes in West Africa: The Case of the Tongo in the Gambia, Guinea, and Sierra Leone." *Society & Natural Resources* 10(4): 383–402.

REFERENCES 125

Freund, B. 1981. *Capital and Labour in the Nigerian Tin Mines*. New Jersey: Humanities Press.

Frey, R. S., Gellert, P. K., and Dahms, H. F. (eds.). 2019. *Ecologically Unequal Exchange: Environmental Injustice in Comparative and Historical Perspective*. London, UK: Palgrave Macmillan.

Frost, D. 2012. *From the Pit to the Market: Politics and the Diamond Economy in Sierra Leone*. UK: James Currey.

Fyfe, C. 1962. *A History of Sierra Leone*. Edinburgh: Oxford University Press.

George, C. 1968. *The rise of British West Africa*. London: Frank Cass & Co. Ltd.

Geschiere, P. 2010 Authochthony: 'Local or Global'? In *Translocality: The Study of Globalizing Processes from a Southern Perspective*, edited by U. Freitag, and A. Von Oppen, 207–228. Leiden, The Netherlands: Brill NV.

Goeury, H. 2021. "Rafael Correa's Decade in Power (2007–2017): Citizens' Revolution, Sumak Kawsay, and Neo-Extractivism in Ecuador." *Latin American Perspectives* 48(3): 206–226. https://doi.org/10.1177/0094582X2110049.

Goucher, C. L. 1981. "Iron Is Iron 'til it is rust: Trade and Ecology in the Decline of West African Smelting." *The Journal of African History* 22(2): 179–189. https://doi.org/10.1017/S0021853700019393.

Govt. of Sierra Leone. 2023. *Mining Agreements*. National Minerals Agency https://www.nma.gov.sl/mining-agreements/.

Govt. of Sierra Leone. 2022a. *The National Land Commission Act, 2022*. Freetown, Sierra Leone.

Govt. of Sierra Leone. 2022b. *The Customary Land Rights Act, 2022*. Freetown, Sierra Leone.

Govt. of Sierra Leone. 2022c. *The Environmental Protection Agency Act, 2022*. Freetown, Sierra Leone.

Govt. of Sierra Leone. 2021. *The Mines and Minerals Development Act, 2021*. Freetown, Sierra Leone.

Govt. of Sierra Leone. 2020. *Republic of Sierra Leone National Action Plan for Reducing Mercury Use in the Artisanal and Small-scale Gold Mining (ASM) Sector in Sierra Leone*. Environment Protection Agency, Freetown, Sierra Leone. https://mercuryconvention.org/sites/default/files/documents/national_action_plan/Sierra-Leone-ASGM-NAP-2020.pdf.

Govt. of Sierra Leone. 2019. *Sierra Leone's Medium-Term National Development Plan 2019–2023: Education for Development*. Freetown, Sierra Leone.

Govt. of Sierra Leone. 2018a. *The Sierra Leone Minerals Policy*. Ministry of Mines and Mineral Resources, November 2018. Freetown, Sierra Leone.

Govt. of Sierra Leone. 2018b. *The Republic of Sierra Leone Artisanal Mining Policy*. Freetown, Sierra Leone. https://www.nma.gov.sl/wp-content/uploads/2019/05/Artisanal-Mining-Policy-for-Sierra-Leone.pdf.

Govt. of Sierra Leone. 2015a. *The Agenda for Prosperity: Sierra Leone's Third Generation Poverty Reduction Strategy Paper (2013–2018)*. http://www.statehouse.gov.sl/images/pics/afp%20version%207.1doc.pdf.

Govt. of Sierra Leone. 2015b. *Ministry of Mines and Mineral Resources*. http://slminerals.org/.

Govt. of Sierra Leone. 2015c. *Final National Land Policy of Sierra Leone, Version 6*. Ministry of Lands, Country Planning and the Environment. FAOLEX Database https://faolex.fao.org/docs/pdf/sie155203.pdf.

126   CULTURE AND CONFLICTS IN SIERRA LEONE MINING

Govt. of Sierra Leone. 2015d. *State House: The Republic of Sierra Leone The role of chiefs is very important in governance—President Koroma.* http://www.statehouse.gov.sl/index. php/component/content/article/34-news-articles/1322-the-role-of-chiefs-is-very-important-in-governance-president-koroma-

Govt. of Sierra Leone. 2014a. *President Ernest Bai Koroma has officially recognized and handed over the symbols of Authority to the newly elected Paramount Chiefs.* http://www.slbc. sl/president-ernest-bai-koroma-has-officially-recognized-and-handed-over-the-symbols-of-authority-to-the-newly-elected-paramount-chiefs/.

Govt. of Sierra Leone. 2014b. SLEITI Holds Re-orientation Workshop on EITI Principles and Process By State House Communications Unit. http://www.statehouse.gov. sl/index.php/component/content/article/34-news-articles/1271-sleiti-holds-re-orientation-workshop-on-eiti-principles-and-process.

Govt. of Sierra Leone. 2009a. *The Mines and Minerals Act 2009.* Freetown: Government Printer.

Govt. of Sierra Leone. 2009b. *The Chieftancy Act 2009.* Freetown: Government Printer.

Govt. of Sierra Leone. 2003. *Statement by his excellency President Ahmad Tejan-Kabbah in Koidu on the occasion of the launching of the Kono Peace Diamond Alliance.* 27 August 2003. http://www.statehouse-sl.org/speeches/kono-diamond-august27.html.

Govt. of Sierra Leone. 2002. *The Sierra Rutile Agreement.* Freetown: Government Printer.

Govt. of Sierra Leone. 1992. *The Bauxite Mineral Prospecting and Mining Agreement, 1992(Ratification) Decree 1992.* Freetown, Sierra Leone.

Govt. of Sierra Leone. 1991. The Constitution of Sierra leone, 1991. www.sierra-leone. org/Laws/constitution1991.pdf.

Govt. of Sierra Leone. 1978. The Constitution of Sierra Leone, 1978. www.sierra-leone. org/Laws/1978-12s.pdf.

Govt. of Sierra Leone. 1972. *Report of the Mines Division of the Ministry of Lands and Mines,1971.* Freetown: Government Printer.

Govt. of Sierra Leone. 1970. *Report of the Mines Division of the Ministry of Lands, Mines and Labour, 1965–1969.* Freetown: Government Printer.

Govt. of Sierra Leone. 1966. Report of the Mines Department, 1964. Freetown: Government Printer.

Govt. of Sierra Leone. 1963. *Report of the Mines Division of the Ministry of Lands, Mines and Labour, 1963.* Freetown: Government Printer.

Govt. of Sierra Leone. 1962. *Report of the Mines Division of the Ministry of Lands, Mines and Labour, 1962.* Freetown: Government Printer.

Govt. of Sierra Leone. 1961. *Report of the Mines Department, 1960.* Government Printer, Freetown.

Govt. of Sierra Leone. 1960a. *Sierra Leone: Annual Report of the Mines Department for the year 1959.* Freetown: Government Printer.

Govt. of Sierra Leone. 1960b. *The Laws of Sierra Leone.* Freetown: Government Printer.

Govt. of Sierra Leone. 1960. Report of the Mines Department, 1959. Government Printer, Freetown.

Govt. of Sierra Leone. 1959. *Report on the Mines Department, 1957.* Freetown: Government Printer.

Govt. of Sierra Leone. 1958a. *Report on the Mines Department, 1956.* Freetown: Government Printer.

Govt. of Sierra Leone. 1958b. *Legislative Council Debates.* Freetown: Government Printer.

REFERENCES   127

Govt. of Sierra Leone. 1957. *1955 Report on the Mines Department*. Freetown: Government Printer.

Govt. of Sierra Leone. 1956. *Interim report on the alluvial diamond mining scheme*. Chief Inspector of Mines, 18 June 1956. Freetown: Government Printer.

Govt. of Sierra Leone. 1955. *Report on the Mines Department for 1953*. Freetown: Government Printing Office.

Govt. of Sierra Leone. 1954. *Report on the Mines Department for 1952*. Freetown: Government Printing Office.

Govt. of Sierra Leone. 1953. *Report on the Mines Department for 1951*. Freetown: Government Printing Office.

Govt. of Sierra Leone. 1952. *Annual Report of the Mines Department for the year 1950*. Freetown: Government Printer.

Govt. of Sierra Leone. 1949. *Colony of Sierra Leone: Annual Report of the Mines Department for the year 1947*. Freetown: Government Printer.

Govt. of Sierra Leone. 1948. *Colony of Sierra Leone: Report of the Mines Department for the year 1945*. Freetown: Government Printer.

Govt. of Sierra Leone. 1946. *Consolidated Report of the Mines Department, 1939 to 1944*. Freetown: Government Printer.

Govt. of Sierra Leone. 1939. Annual Report of the Geological and Mines Department for the year 1938. Freetown: Government Printer, 1939.

Govt. of Sierra Leone. 1938. *Tribal Authorities Ordinance 1938*. http://www.sierra-leone. org/Laws/Cap%2061.pdf.

Govt. of Sierra Leone. 1937. *Sierra Leone: Annual Report of the Geological and Mines Department for the year 1936*. Freetown: Government Printer.

Govt. of Sierra Leone. 1936. *Sierra Leone: Reports of the Geological and Mines Department for the years 1935 and 1934*. Freetown: Government Printer.

Govt. of Sierra Leone 1935. *Sierra Leone: Annual Reports of the Geological and Mines Department for the years 1933 and 1934*. Freetown: Government Printer.

Govt. of Sierra Leone. 1934. *Sierra Leone: Report of the Geological and Mines Department for the year 1932*. Freetown: Government Printer.

Govt. of Sierra Leone. 1932. *Report of the Geological and Mines Department for the years 1930 and 1931*. Freetown: Government Printer.

Govt. of Sierra Leone. 1930. *Report of the Geological Department for the year 1929*. Freetown: Government Printer.

Govt. of Sierra Leone. 1929. *Sierra Leone: Report of the Geological Department for part of the year 1927 and for the year 1928*. Freetown: Government Printer.

Govt. of Sierra Leone. 1921. *Report of the Geological Survey for the year 1921*. Freetown: Government Printing Office.

Grätz, T., and Werthmann, K. (eds.). 2012. *Mining Frontiers in Africa: Anthropological and Historical Perspectives (Mainzer Beiträge zur Afrikaforschung)*. Koln, Germany: Rüdiger Köpp.

Greco, E. 2020. "Africa, Extractivism and the Crisis this Time." *Review of African Political Economy*, 47(166): 511–521. https://doi.org/10.1080/03056244.2020.1859839.

Gudykunst, W. B. 1983. "Toward a Typology of Stranger-Host Relationships." *International Journal of Intercultural Relations* 7:401–413. https://doi.org/10.1016/0147-1767(83)90046-9.

Gudynas, E. 2016. "Beyond Varieties of Development: Disputes and Alternatives." *Third World Quarterly* 37(4): 721–732. https://doi.org/10.1080/01436597.2015.1126504.

Hall, T. D., and Fenelon, J. V. 2015. *Indigenous Peoples and Globalization: Resistance and Revitalization*. London: Routledge.

Hall, S. 1996. New Ethnicities. In *Black British Cultural Studies: A Reader*, edited by H. A. Baker, M. Diawara, and R. H. Lindeborg, 163–172. Chicago: University of Chicago Press.

Harbottle, M. 1976. *The Knaves of Diamonds*. London: Seely Service.

Harding, A. 2022. "Legislators Debate the Customary Land Right Act 2022." *The Calabash Newspaper*, August 1, 2022. https://thecalabashnewspaper.com/legislators-debate-the-customary-land-right-act-2022/.

Hargreaves, J. D. 1956. "The establishment of Sierra Leone." *Cambridge Historical Journal* 12(1) 1956 Kraus Reprint Company/ and Cambridge University Press 56, 57–66. In *Nineteenth-Century Africa*. London: Oxford University Press.

Harris, W. T. 1954. "Ceremonies and Stories Connected with Trees, Rivers and Hills in the Protectorate of Sierra Leone." In *Sierra Leone Studies*, edited by J. D. Hargreaves. New Series No. 2 (pp. 91–97). Great Britain: Steven Austin and Sons Ltd. Oriental and General Printers.

Hauser, J. M. 2013. "From DELCO Road to Marampa Pub and Back: Austria at Marampa Mines, 1980–1985." Masters Thesis, University of Birmingham, UK.

Hayward, F. M. 1972. "The Development of a Radical Political Organization in the Bush: A Case Study in Sierra Leone." *Canadian Journal of African Studies* 6(1): 1–28. https://doi.org/10.1080/00083968.1972.10803654.

Hechter, M. 2000. *Containing Nationalism*. New York: Oxford University Press.

Heilmann, J. 2007. "Sierra Leone Police Open Fire on Locals Protesting Mining Practices." Voice of America, 14 December, 2007. http://www.voanews.com.

Hilson, G., Hilson, A., Maconachie, R. McQuilken, J., and Goumandakoye, H. 2017. "Artisanal and Small-scale Mining (ASM) in Sub-Saharan Africa: Re-conceptualizing Formalization and 'Illegal' Activity." *Geoforum* 83: 80–90. https://doi.org/10.1016/j.geoforum.2017.05.004.

Hirsch J. L. 2001. *Sierra Leone Diamonds and the Struggle for Democracy*. International Peace Academy Occasional Paper Series. London: Lynne Rienner Publishers.

Hoogvelt, A. M. M., and Tinker, A. M. 1978. "The Role of Colonial and Post-colonial States in Imperialism: A Case Study of Sierra Leone." *The Journal of Modern African Studies* 16(1): 67–79. https://doi.org/10.1017/S0022278X00007825.

Hughes Jennett, J., and Hood, P. 2020. "Kalma v African Minerals: English Court of Appeal Judgment Cuts Against the Grain of Common Law Cases on the Responsibility of Businesses for Overseas Human Rights Impacts." *EJIL: Talk! Blog of the European Journal of International Law* March 24, 2020. https://www.ejiltalk.org/kalma-v-african-minerals-court-of-appeal-judgment-cuts-against-the-grain-of-common-law-cases-on-the-responsibility-of-businesses-for-overseas-human-rights-impacts/.

Human Rights Watch. 2014. "Whose Development? Human Rights Abuses in Sierra Leone's Mining Boom." https://www.hrw.org/report/2014/02/19/whose-development/human-rights-abuses-sierra-leones-mining-boom.

Hunter, M., and Smith, A. 2017. "Follow the Money: Financial Flows Linked to Artisanal and Small-scale Gold Mining in Sierra Leone: A Case Study." Global Initiative Against Transnational Organized Crime, Levin Sources, and GIZ.

Ibrahim-Fofana, A., Blair, R., and Buss, D. 2020. "Gendered 'choices' in Sierra Leone: Women in Artisanal Mining in Tonkolili District." *Canadian Journal of African Studies/*

REFERENCES

Revue canadienne des études africaines, 54(1): 157–176. https://doi.org/10.1080/0008396
8.2019.1671207.

Ibrahim-Fofana, A. 2019. "The Bondo Society as a Political Tool: Examining Cultural Expertise in Sierra Leone from 1961 to 2018." *Laws* 8(3): 17. https://doi.org/10.3390/laws8030017.

IEA. 2023. Final List of Critical Minerals 2022. International Energy Agency. https://www.iea.org/policies/15271-final-list-of-critical-minerals-2022.

Invest Salone. 2022. "Proposed Customary Land Reform under the Private Sector Spotlight." 27 April 2022. https://investsalone.com/news/proposed-customary-land-reform-under-the-private-sector-spotlight/.

Irish University Press. 1968. "Irish University Press Series of British Parliamentary Papers Colonies, Africa" vol. 5 Session 1865.

Jacket Media Co. 2021. "African Nations Partner With NASA to Fight Illegal Mining." https://jacketmediaco.com/african-nations-partner-with-nasa-to-fight-illegal-mining-2/.

Jackson, M. 2011. *Life within Limits: Well-being in a World of Want*. Durham, NC: Duke University Press.

Jackson P. 2006. "Reshuffling an Old Deck of Cards? The Politics of Local Government Reform in Sierra Leone." *African Affairs* 106(422): 95–111.

Jalloh, A. 2018. *Muslim Fula Business Elites and Politics in Sierra Leone*. Rochester, NY: University of Rochester Press.

James, L. D. 1965. "Regional Geochemical Reconnaissance in the Northern and Southern Sections of the Sula Mountains Schist Belt, Sierra Leone." Ph.D. diss., University of London.

Jedrej M. C. 1974. "An Analytical Note on the Land and Spirits of the Sewa Mende." *Africa* 44: 38–45. https://doi.org/10.2307/1158565.

Jorgenson, A. K., and Clark, B. 2012. "Footprints: The Division of Nations and Nature." In *Ecology and Power: Struggles Over Land and Material Resources in the Past, Present, and Future*, edited by A. Hornborg, B. Clark, and K. Hermele, 155–167. London: Routledge.

Kabba, A. 2010. "African Minerals Compensates Land Owners." *Sierra Express Media*, 9 June 2010. https://sierraexpressmedia.com/?p=9837.

Kamara, S. 1997. "Mined out: 'The environmental and social implications of development finance to rutile mining in Sierra Leone.'" *Friend of the Earth Trust*, April 1997. www.foe.co.uk/pubsinfo/briefings/html/19971215144610.html.

Kaplan, I., Dobert, M., McLaughlin, J. L., Marvin, B. J., and Whitaker, D. P. 1976. *Area Handbook for Sierra Leone*. DA Pam 550–180. Foreign Area Studies. Washington, DC: American University.

Keili, A. K. 1993. "Environmental Issues of Mining in Sierra Leone." Report to the Ministry of Lands, Housing and the Environment, Freetown, Sierra Leone.

King N. 2007. Conflict as integration: Youth aspiration to personhood in the teleology of Sierra leone's senseless war. *Current African Issues* 36, Uppsala: Nordiska Afrikainstitutet.

Knight Piesold and Co. 2001. "Sierra Rutile Limited environmental and social assessment, Project 1807A." Prepared for Sierra Rutile Limited, Freetown Sierra Leone. Denver, CO: Knight Piesold and Co.

Konneh, A. 1996. Citizenship at the Margins: Status, Ambiguity and Mandingo of Liberia. *African Studies Review* 39(2): 141–154. https://doi.org/10.2307/525439.

Korzeniewicz, R. P. 2018. *The World-System as Unit of Analysis: Past Contributions and Future Advances*. New York: Routledge.

KPCSC. 2020. "NMJD's Press Release on Court Order Freezing Assets of Diamond Miner Octea in Sierra Leone." *Kimberley Process Civil Society Coalition.* https://www.kpcivilsociety.org/press/nmjds-press-release-on-freezing-order-on-assets-of-diamond-miner-octea-in-sierra-leone/.

Labi, M. L. C. 1972. "Politics in an African Mining Community." Ph.D. diss., University of Pittsburgh.

Lahai Samboma, J. 2019. "Sierra Leone: Local Population Doesn't Benefit from Diamond Industry Due to Corruption & Smuggling, Says Analyst." *Africa Business Magazine,* 7 May 2019. https://www.business-humanrights.org/en/latest-news/sierra-leone-local-population-doesnt-benefit-from-diamond-industry-due-to-corruption-smuggling-says-analyst/.

Lamin A. S., Akiwumi, F., Conteh, M. A. R., and Sannoh, W. B. 1991. "Water Balance of the Sierra Rutile Mining Area; water year May 1990 to April 1991." Consultancy Report by Environmental and Scientific Consulting Group (ESCG).

Leach, M. 1994. *Rainforest Relations: Gender and Resource Use among the Mende of Gola, Sierra Leone.* Washington, DC: Smithsonian Institution Press.

Lebbie, A. R., and Freudenberger, M. S. 1996. "Sacred Groves in Africa: Forest Patches in Transition." In *Forest Patches in Tropical Landscapes,* edited by J. Schelhas, and R. Greenberg, 300–324.Washington, DC: Island Press.

Lentz, C. 2013. *Land, Mobility, and Belonging in West Africa: Natives and Strangers.* Indiana: Indiana University Press.

Levin, E. A., and Turay, A. B. 2008. "Artisanal Diamond Cooperatives in Sierra Leone: Success or Failure." *Africa Portal.* https://www.africaportal.org/publications/artisanal-diamond-cooperatives-in-sierra-leone-success-or-failure/.

Levin, E. A., and Gberie, L. 2006. "Dealing for Development? A Study of Diamond Marketing and Pricing in Sierra Leone." *Africa Portal.* https://www.africaportal.org/publications/the-dynamics-of-diamond-pricing-and-marketing-in-sierra-leone/.

Levine, D. N. 1977. "Simmel at a Distance: On the History and Systematics of the Sociology of the Stranger." *Sociological Focus* 10(1): 15–29. https://doi.org/10.1080/00380237.1977.10570274.

Lewis, R. 1954. "Sierra Leone: A Modern Portrait." London: Her Majesty's Stationary Office.

Li, M. 2021. "China: Imperialism or Semi-Periphery?" *Monthly Review* 73(3): 47–74.

Mabey, P. T., Li, W., Sundufi, A. J., and Lashari, A. H. 2020. "Environmental Impacts: 5525. https://doi.org/10.3390/su12145525.

Maconachie, R. and Hilson, G. 2016. "Re-Thinking the Child Labor "Problem" in Rural Sub-Saharan Africa: The Case of Sierra Leone's Half Shovels." *World Development* 78: 136–147.

Maconachie, R., and Hilson, G. 2011. "Artisanal Gold Mining: A New Frontier in Post-Conflict Sierra Leone?" *The Journal of Development Studies* 47(4): 595–616. https://doi.org/10.1080/00220381003599402.

Mamdani, M. 2000. "Culture and Human Rights: Orientalising, Occcidentalising and Authenticity." In *Beyond Rights Talks and Culture Talk: Comparative Essays on the Politics of Rights and Cultures,* edited by M. Mamdani, 15–36. NY: St Martin's Press.

Mamdani, M. 1996. *Citizen and Subject: Contemporary Africa and the Legacy of Late Colonialism.* NJ: Princeton University Press.

Mannathukkaren, N. 2010. "Postcolonialism and Modernity: A Critical Realist Critique." *Journal of Critical Realism* 9(3): 299–327.

REFERENCES

131

Mansaray, J. 2006. "Sierra Leone Rutile in Big Land Scam." *Awareness Times, Sierra Leone News and Information*, Nov 8, 2006.

Mapara, J. 2009. Indigenous Knowledge Systems in Zimbabwe: Juxtaposing Postcolonial Theory. *The Journal of Pan African Studies* 3(1): 139–155.

Marcantonio, R., and Fuentes, A. 2020. "A Clear Past and a Murky Future: Life in the Anthropocene on the Pampana River, Sierra Leone." *Land* 9(3): 1–17. https://doi.org/10.3390/land9030072.

Margao, P. J. 2021. "Assessing the Challenges of Diamond Mining and Its Impact on Sierra Leone's Economy." MA Thesis. International Institute of Social Studies, The Hague, The Netherlands.

Marrah, S. 2022. "Illegal Mining Suspect Released on Bail." *Politico SL Online*, 15/06/22. https://politicosl.com/articles/illegal-mining-suspect-released-bail.

Massaquoi, M., and Hill K. 2008. "Rutile Disaster Blamed on Neglect." *Concord Times* July 30, 2008. https://allafrica.com/stories/200807300557.html.

Mather, A. L. 1959. "Geochemical Prospecting Studies in Sierra Leone." Ph.D. diss., Imperial College London.

McClanahan, P. 2010. "Massive Iron Ore Project Brings Mining Tensions Back to Sierra Leone." *The Christian Science Monitor*. https://www.csmonitor.com/World/Africa/Africa-Monitor/2010/1212/Massive-iron-ore-project-brings-mining-tensions-back-to-Sierra-Leone.

Mckenzie, D. H. 1963. "Geology of the Gbangbama Area." Bulletin No. 3 of the Geological Survey Division, Freetown, Sierra Leone.

Metcalfe, G. E. 1964. *Great Britain and Ghana: Documents of Ghana History 1807–1957*. London: Thomas Nelson and Sons Ltd.

Mining Journal. 2018. "Sierra Leone: Promise to Prosperity." *Mining Journal*. https://www.mining-journal.com/digital_assets/469c0ca1-38de-43bd-af37-a4d5cf503844/Sierra_Leone_2018scr_v2.pdf.

Mining Technology. 2021. Tonkolili Iron Ore Mine, Sierra Leone, West Africa. UK-based African Minerals (AML) through its subsidiary Tonkolili Iron Ore, is developing the Tonkolili iron ore mine in Sierra Leone, West Africa. June 11, 2021. https://www.mining-technology.com/projects/tonkolili-iron-ore-mine/.

Mitchell, H. 2002. *Remote Corners: A Sierra Leone Memoir*. London, UK: The Radcliffe Press.

Moore, H. L., and Sanders, T. 2001. "Magical Interpretations and Material Realities: An Introduction." In *Magical Interpretations and Material Realities: Modernity, Witchcraft and the Occult in Postcolonial Africa*, edited by H. L. Moore, and T. Sanders, 1–27. USA: Routledge.

Mouser, B. L. 1980. "Accommodation and Assimilation in the Landlord-Stranger Relationship." In *West African Culture Dynamics: Archaeological and Historical Perspectives*, edited by B. K. Swartz, and R. E. Dummett, 495–514. The Hague: Mouton.

NAMATI. 2022. "Sierra Leone Enacts Unprecedented Laws Related to Land, Climate, and Sustainable Development." https://namati.org/news-stories/sierra-leone-enacts-unprecedented-laws-related-to-land-climate-sustainable-development/.

Njini, F., Cohen, M., and Kavanagh, M. J. 2020. "Gold Production Decline; Sierra Leone Smuggling: Mining Update." *Bloomberg Financial Post*. February, 4, 2020. https://www.bloomberg.com/news/articles/2020-02-04/anglo-ceo-praises-brutally-honest-eskom-boss-mining-update#xj4y7vzkg.

Njoh, A. J. 2006. *Tradition Culture and Development in Africa*. Vermont: Ashgate.

132 CULTURE AND CONFLICTS IN SIERRA LEONE MINING

Nzongola-Ntalaja, G. 2007. "The Politics of Citizenship in the Democratic Republic of Congo." In *Making Nations, Creating Strangers: States and Citizenship in Africa* edited by S. Dorman, D. Hammett, and P. Nugent, 69–82. Leiden: Brill.

Obeng-Odoom, F. 2015a. "Understanding Land Grabs in Africa: Insights from Marxist and Georgist Political Economics." *The Review of Black Political Economy* 42(4): 337–354.

Obeng-Odoom, F. 2015b. "Africa's Development post 2015: A Critical Defence of Postcolonial Thinking." *Journal of Pan African Studies* 8(1): 37–45.

Ochiai, T. 2017. "A Historical Overview of Local Government in the Protectorate of Sierra Leone." 2017/06/26 DISCUSSION PAPERS. http://www.shd.chiba-u.jp/glblcrss/Discussion_Papers/pdf/Local_Government_in_Sierra_Leone.pdf.

Ojukutu Macauley, S., and Keili A. K. 2008. "Citizens, Subjects or a Dual Mandate? Artisanal Miners, Supporters and the Resource Scramble in Sierra Leone." *Development Southern Africa* 25(5): 513–530. https://doi.org/10.1080/03768350802447610.

Panella, C. 2010. "Gold Mining in West Africa: Worlds of Debts and Sites of Co-habitation." In *Worlds of Debt: Interdisciplinary Perspectives on Gold Mining in West Africa*, edited by C. Panella, 1–14. Amsterdam: Rozenberg Publishers.

Partnership Canada Africa. 2004. *Rich man, Poor Man Development Diamonds and Poverty Diamond: The Potential for Change in the Alluvial Diamond Fields of Africa*. Ontario, CA: Global Witness Publishing Inc.

The Patriotic Vanguard. 2013a. "London Mining Responds to Open Letter from Lunsar Descendants." 24 July 2013. http://www.thepatrioticvanguard.com/london-mining-responds-to-open-letter-from-lunsar-descendants.

The Patriotic Vanguard. 2013b. "Open Letter to London Mining-Sierra Leone." 12 July 2013. http://thepatrioticvanguard.com/open-letter-to-london-mining-sierra-leone.

Peltier, E. 2022. "New Laws of the Land: Sierra Leone Reshapes Environmental Battleground." *New York Times*. 9 August 2022. https://www.nytimes.com/2022/08/09/world/africa/sierra-leone-land-environment.html.

Perinbam, B. M. 1988. "The Political Organization of Traditional Gold Mining: The Western Loby, c. 1850 to c. 1910." *The Journal of African History* 29(3): 437–462. https://doi.org/10.1017/S0021853700030577.

Perinbam, B. M. 1980. "The Jules in Western Sudan history: Long-distance Traders and Developers of Resources." In *West African Culture Dynamics: Archaeological and Historical Perspectives*, edited by B. K. Swartz, and R. E. Dumett, 455–476. Great Britain: Mouton Publishers.

Peters, K. 2011. *"War and the Crisis of Youth in Sierra Leone."* New York: Cambridge University Press.

Peters, P. E. 2004. "Inequality and Social Conflict over Land in Africa." *Journal of Agrarian Change* 4: 269–314. https://doi.org/10.1111/j.1471-0366.2004.00080.x.

Phillips, R. B. 1995. *Representing Woman: Sande Masquerades of the Mende of Sierra Leone*. Los Angeles CA: UCLA Fowler Museum of Cultural History.

Pijpers, R. 2014. "Crops and Carats: Exploring the Interconnectedness of Mining and Agriculture in Sub-Saharan Africa." *Futures* 62: 32–39. https://doi.org/10.1016/j.futures.2014.01.012.

Prichard, W. 2013. "Building a Fair, Transparent and Inclusive Tax System in Sierra Leone." *Tax Justice Network Africa/BAN/NACE*. http://www.nacesl.org/SaloneReport_Final%20print%20out.pdf.

REFERENCES
133

Rashid I. 2004. Student Radicals, Lumpen Youth, and the Origins of the Revolutionary United Front (RUF/SL). In *Between Democracy and Terror: The Sierra Leone Civil War,* edited by I. Abdullah, 66–89. Dakar: CODESRIA.

Reeck, D. L. 1976. *Deep Mende: Religious Interactions in a Changing African Rural Society.* Leiden: Brill.

Remoe, V. 2023. "Minister of Mines Uses New Customary Land Laws to Get More For Rural Landowners." https://vickieremoe.com/blog/2023/2/6/a-better-deal-and-a-new-direction-for-sierra-leone-mining. https://vickieremoe.com/blog/2023/2/6/a-better-deal-and-a-new-direction-for-sierra-leone-mining.

Remoe, V. 2013. "For Noncompliance Extractive Industries Transparency Board Suspends Sierra Leone." *Global Times.*

Renner-Thomas, A. 2010. *Land Tenure in Sierra Leone: The Law, Dualism and the Making of a Land Policy.* UK: AuthorHouse, UK.

Reno, W. 1995. *Corruption and State Politics in Sierra Leone.* Cambridge: Cambridge University Press.

Reuters. 2018. "Iluka Resumes Operations at Sierra Leone Rutile Mine as Strike Ends." *Reuters,* 1 December 2018. https://www.reuters.com/article/us-iluka-leone-strike/iluka-resumes-operations-at-sierra-leone-rutile-mine-as-strike-ends-idUSKCN1O03LC.

Rice, J. 2007. "Ecological Unequal Exchange: International Trade and Uneven Utilization of Environmental Space in the World-System." *Social Forces* 85(3): 1369–1392. https://doi.org/10.1353/sof.2007.0054.

Richards P. 2005. "To Fight or to Farm? Agrarian dimensions of the Mano River Conflicts (Liberia and Sierra Leone)." *African Affairs* 104(417): 571–590.

Richards, P. 2002. *Fighting for the Rainforest: War, Youth and Resources in Sierra Leone.* London: The International African Institute, in association with James Currey and Heinemann.

Richards, P. 1986. *Coping with Hunger: Experiment and Hazard in an African Farming System.* London, England: Allen & Unwin.

Rodney, W. 1981. *How Europe Underdeveloped Africa.* Washington, DC: Howard University Press.

Rogers, E. M. 1999. "Georg Simmel's Concept of the Stranger and Intercultural Communication Research." *Communication Theory* 9(1): 58–74. https://doi.org/10.1111/j.1468-2885.1999.tb00162.x.

Rose, P. I. 1967. "Strangers in Their Midst: Small-town Jews and Their Neighbors." In *The Study of Society,* edited by P. I. Rose, 463–479. New York: Random House.

Rosen, D. M. 1981. "Dangerous Women: Ideology, Knowledge and Ritual among the Kono of Eastern Sierra Leone." *Dialectical Anthropology* 6(2): 151–163. https://www.jstor.org/stable/29790029.

Rosen, D. M. 1973. "Diamonds, Diggers, and Chiefs: The Politics of Fragmentation in a West African Society." Ph.D. diss., University of Illinois.

Samba, A. 2012. "In Sierra Leone, London Mining Rescues Central Business District of Lunsar." *Awareness Times.* http://news.sl/drwebsite/publish/article_200519495.shtml.

Samura, J. 2021. "Minister of Mines Launches Wongor's Gold Processing Plant." National Minerals Agency. https://www.nma.gov.sl/minister-of-mines-launches-wongors-gold-processing-plant/.

134   CULTURE AND CONFLICTS IN SIERRA LEONE MINING

Savino, L. 2016. "Landscapes of Contrast: The Neo-extractivist State and Indigenous Peoples in 'Post-neoliberal' Argentina." *The Extractive Industries and Society*, 3(2): 404–415. https://doi.org/10.1016/j.exis.2016.02.011.

Sawyerr, H. 1970. *God, Ancestor or Creator?: Aspects of Traditional Belief in Ghana, Nigeria & Sierra Leone.* London: Longman.

Sawyerr, H. 1968. "The Practice of Presence." *Numen* 15(2): 142–161. https://doi.org/10.2307/3269780.

Saylors, R. G. 1967. *The Economic System of Sierra Leone.* Durham, NC: Duke University Press.

Schwartz, P. 2006. *Sustainable Development and Mining in Sierra Leone.* Kent, UK: Pnuema Spring.

Segkoma G. A. 1986. "The History of Mining and Agriculture in Sierra Leone: A Study of the Impact of Some Aspects of Colonial and Post-colonial Government's Economic Policies, 1929–1982." Unpublished Ph.D. diss., Dalhousie University.

Seibure, I., and Hill, K. 2008. "Sierra Rutile Tops Government Mining Review." *Concord Times* 26 May 2008 https://allafrica.com/stories/200805270484.html.

Sesay, O. K. 2023. "Lake Sonfon." https://independent.academia.edu/OluKomborSesay.

Sesay, L. J. 2008. "Disaster at Sierra Rutile." *The Patriotic Vanguard*, 29 July 2008. http://www.thepatrioticvanguard.com/disaster-at-sierra-rutile.

Shack, W. A., and Skinner, E. P. 1979. *Strangers in African Societies.* Berkeley, CA: University of California Press.

Sheriff, F. 2022. "Sierra Leone: Environment—Impacts of Illegal Mining Activities: Threat to Water Security, Human Health, and Potential National Public Health Emergency." *Concord Times (Freetown)*, 9 August 2022. https://allafrica.com/stories/202208090226.html.

Sierra Express Media (S.E.M.). 2011. "President Koroma Presents New Staffs To 149 Paramount Chiefs In Salone." https://sierraexpressmedia.com/?p=22914.

Sierra Express Media (S.E.M.). 2009. "70%-75% of the new mining act is good for Sierra Leone but implementation is the problem says lawyer Pa-Momo Fofanah." https://sierraexpressmedia.com/?p=4675.

Sierra Leone Development Co Ltd. 1944. "Government Post-War African Housing Policy" London: The National Archives, 32199/4.

Sierra Leone Govt Papers. 1882. "Correspondence respecting the proceedings at the Jong River in May 1882." London: George E. B. Eyre & William Spottiswoode.

Sierra Leone Web. 2023. "The Minerals Ordinance 1927." http://www.sierra-leone.org/Laws/Cap%20196.pdf.

Sierra Loaded. 2022. Sierra Leone's President Julius Maada Bio Recognises and Coronates Eight New Paramount Chiefs, Encourages Them to Be Peace Ambassadors. 12 June 2022.

Sierra Rutile Ltd. 2003a. "Letter from Landowner's Federation president to Paramount Chief of Lower Banta." 13 September 2003.

Sierra Rutile Ltd. 2023b. LinkedIn Posting: https://ao.linkedin.com/posts/sierra-rutile-limited_ninety-ninestudents-from-the-five-mining-activity-6985939042500509697-Du8z.

Sierra Rutile Ltd. 2023c. LinkedIn Posting: https://ao.linkedin.com/posts/sierra-rutile-limited_mining-africa-sierraleone-activity-6971301858548072448-wZZD.

Simas, M., Wood, R., and Hertwich, E. 2015. "Labor Embodied in Trade: The Role of Labor and Energy Productivity and Implications for Greenhouse Gas Emissions." *Journal of Industrial Ecology* 19(3): 343–356. https://doi.org/10.1111/jiec.12187.

REFERENCES   135

Smith, C., and Ward, G. (eds.). 2000. *Indigenous Cultures in an Interconnected World*. Vancouver: UBC Press.

Squire, C. B., and Sannoh, W. 1994. "Monitoring disposal procedures for noxious tailings from Sierra Rutile Limited's operating plants." Project Proposal for Sierra Rutile Limited.

Squire, C. B. 1993. "Environmental assessment of SRL effluents and noxious tailings." Department of Chemistry, Department of Environmental Sciences, Njala University College, University of Sierra Leone, PMB, Freetown.

SRK Consulting. 2018a. "Sierra Rutile Expansion Area 1—Environmental, Social and Health Impact Assessment Social Impact Assessment." Report Number 515234/SIA/Final.

SRK Consulting. 2018b. "Sierra Rutile Project Area 1—Environmental, Social and Health Impact Assessment: Mine Closure Plan" Report Number: 515234/Mine Closure Plan.

Standard-Times. 2008. "Sierra Rutile Ltd.: Working for a better Sierra Leone." October 17, 2008.

Steel. R. W. 2001. *Sierra Leone 1938: Journey through a Vanishing World*. Oxon, UK: Ituri Publications.

Stonequist, E. 1937. *The Marginal Man*. New York: Scribner's.

Sutherland, A. 1977. "Sierra Leone and the 'Stranger Problem.'" *Journal of the Anthropological Society of Oxford* 8(1): 17–24. https://www.anthro.ox.ac.uk/sites/default/files/anthro/documents/media/jaso8_1_1977_17_24.pdf.

Svampa, M. 2019. "Neo-extractivism in Latin America: Socio-environmental Conflicts, the Territorial Turn, and New Political Narratives." In *Elements in Politics and Society in Latin America*, 1–57. Cambridge: Cambridge University Press.

Sylvain, R. 2015. "Foragers and Fictions in the Kalahari: Indigenous Identities and the Politics of Deconstruction." *Anthropological Theory* 15(2): 158–178. https://doi.org/10.1177/146349961456475.

The African World, West Africa. 1937. "Discovery of Diamonds in Sierra Leone: Major Junner gives the Facts." November 13, 1937, p. 187.

The Eagle. 1992. "Diamond Boom in Kono" *Eagle Newspaper*, May 27–3 June 1992, pp 4.

The London Times. 1957. "Call for Sierra Leone Inquiry, Petition by Chiefs." *The London Times*, 2 Nov 1957:6.

The Organizer.net. 2019. "Chinese Nationals Express Shock for their Arrest for Illegal Mining in Sierra Leone." Press release 21/04/19. https://theorganiser.net/world/316-12-chinese-nationals-express-shock-for-their-arrest-for-illegal-mining-in-sierra-leone.

Thomas, A. R. 2023. "Sierra Leone Government Signs Railway Development Agreement with ARISE Integrated Industrial Platform Ltd." *Sierra Leone Telegraph*, 22 January 2023. https://www.thesierraleonetelegraph.com/sierra-leone-government-signs-railway-development-agreement-with-arise-integrated-industrial-platform-ltd/.

Thomas, A. R. 2021a. "Massive Illegal Chinese Goldmining Uncovered in Eastern Sierra Leone." *Sierra Leone Telegraph*, 20June 2021 https://www.thesierraleonetelegraph.com/massive-illegal-chinese-goldmining-uncovered-in-eastern-sierra-leone/.

Thomas, A. R. 2021b. "Magistrate Brima-Jah remands 4 Ghanaian Citizens and 3 others for illegal mining." *Sierra Leone Telegraph*, 9 November 2021 https://www.thesierraleonetelegraph.com/magistrate-brima-jah-remands-4-ghanaian-citizens-and-3-others-for-illegal-mining/.

136   CULTURE AND CONFLICTS IN SIERRA LEONE MINING

Thompson, G. E. 1969. *The Palm Land or West Africa Illustrated: Being a History of Missionary Labors and Travels, with Descriptions of Men and Things in Western Africa. Also, a Synopsis of all the Missionary Work on that Continent.* London: Dawsons of Pall Mall.

Thompson, G. E. 1852. *Thompson in Africa: An Account of the Missionary Labors, Sufferings, Travels, and Observations of George Thompson in Western Africa at the Mendi Mission.* New York: S. W. Benedict.

Thrift, N., and Taylor, M. (eds.). 2013. *Multinationals and the Restructuring of the World Economy: The Geography of Multinationals*, Vol. 2. New York: Routledge.

Timberlake, Lloyd. 1985. *Africa in Crisis: The Causes, The Cure of Environmental Bankruptcy.* London, UK: Earthscan.

UNECA. 1969. "Report on Mining Agreements and Mining Policy in Sierra Leone." United Nations Economic Commission for Africa, M69-2231, Addis Ababa, Ethiopia.

UNESC-ECA. 1968a. "Aspects of works of British government institutions in the evaluation of the newer minerals." In: United Nations Economic And Social Council, Economic Commission For Africa: Seminar on New Metals and Minerals. Addis Ababa 5–10 February 1968. http://repository.uneca.org/bitstream/handle/10855/12287/Bib53339.pdf?sequence=1.

UNESC-ECA. 1968b. "Titanium minerals in Sierra Leone. united nations economic and social council: economic commission for africa." In: United Nations Economic and Social Council, Economic Commission for Africa: Seminar on New Metals and Minerals. Addis Ababa 5–10 February, 1968. http://repository.uneca.org/bitstream/ha.

UNDP. 2012. "Deputy Minister Urges Paramount Chiefs to 'Strive to Become Modern Chiefs of the 21st Century'." Press Release 14 August 2012. http://www.sl.undp.org/content/sierraleone/en/home/presscenter/pressreleases/2012/08/14/deputy-minister-urges-paramount-chiefs-to-strive-to-become-modern-chiefs-of-the-21st-century.

United States Govt. 2023. U.S. Department of Energy Releases 2023 Critical Materials Assessment to Evaluate Supply Chain Security for Clean Energy Technologies. Office of Energy Efficiency & Renewable Energy, July 31, 2023. https://www.energy.gov/eere/articles/us-department-energy-releases-2023-critical-materials-assessment-evaluate-supply.

Unruh, J. D. 2008. "Land Policy Reform, Customary Rule of Law and the Peace Process in Sierra Leone." *African Journal of Legal Studies* 2: 94–117. https://doi.org/10.1163/221097312X13397499736507.

Utas, M. (ed.). 2012. *African Conflicts and Informal Power: Big Men and Networks.* London, UK: Zed Books.

Van der Laan, H. L. 1965. *The Sierra Leone Diamonds: An Economic Study Covering the Years 1952–1961.* Oxford, UK: Oxford University Press.

Vandy, J. 2021. "Government Conducts Massive Raid on Illegal Foreign Miners." Strategic Communications Unit, Ministry of Information and Communications, 23 March 2021. https://mic.gov.sl/Media/News/government-conducts-massive-raid-on-illegal-foreign-miners.

Verma, R. 2014. "Land Grabs, Power, and Gender in East and Southern Africa: So, What's New?" *Feminist Economics* 20(1): 52–75. https://doi.org/10.1080/13545701.2014.897739.

Villa, S. 2018. "Sierra Leone News: Police call for 38 illegal Chinese miners to be deported." *Awoko Newspaper*, 26 September 2018. https://awokonewspaper.sl/sierra-leone-news-police-call-for-38-illegal-chinese-miners-to-be-deported/.

REFERENCES

Villalba-Eguiluz, C. U., and Etxano, I. 2017. "Buen Vivir vs Development (II): The Limits of (Neo-) Extractivism." *Ecological Economics* 138: 1–11. https://doi.org/10.1016/j.ecolecon.2017.03.010.

Villegas, C., Turay, A. B., and Sarmu, D. 2013. "Can Artisanal Mining and Conservation Co-exist? A Case Study of Artisanal Gold & Diamond Mining in and Adjacent to Sierra Leone's Gola Rainforest National Park and Recommendations on the Way Forward." Artisanal and Small-scale Mining in Protected areas and critical Ecosystems programme. WWF-World Wide Fund for Nature and Estelle Levin Ltd.

von Benda-Beckmann, F. 1997. "Citizens, Strangers and Indigenous Peoples: Conceptual Politics and Legal Pluralism: Natural Resources, Environment, and Legal Pluralism." In *Law and Anthropology Vol. 9*, edited by R. Kuppe, and R. Potz, 1–42. The Hague, The Netherlands: Kluwer Law International, Martinus Nijhoff Publishers.

Waldock, E. A., Capstick, E. S., and Browning, A. J. 1951. "Soil Conservation and Land Use in Sierra Leone." Sessional Paper no. 1 of 1951. Freetown, Sierra Leone: Government Printer.

Wallerstein, I. 2000. "Introduction to Special Issue on Commodity Chains in the World Economy, 1590–1790." *Review* 23(1): 1–13.

Wallerstein, I. 1983. *Historical Capitalism*. London: Verso Press.

Welthungerhilfe-SLE. 2012. "Increasing Pressure for Land: Implications for Rural Livelihoods and Development Actors. A Case Study in Sierra Leone." Bonn and Berlin: Deutsche Welthungerhilfe. http://www.nachdenkseiten.de/upload/pdf/Study_Land_Investment_Sierra_Leone.pdf.

Werthmann, K. 2006. "Gold Diggers, Earth Priests and District Heads: Land Rights and Gold Mining in Southwestern Burkina Faso." In *Land and the Politics of Belonging in West Africa*, edited by R. Kuba, and C. Lentz, 199–236. Leiden, The Netherlands: Brill N.V.

Williams, P., and Chrisman, L. (Eds.). 1994. *Colonial Discourse and Postcolonial Theory: A Reader*. New York: Columbia University Press.

Williford, B. 2018. "Buen Vivir as Policy: Challenging Neoliberalism or Consolidating State Power in Ecuador." *Journal of World-systems Research* 24(1): 96–122. https://doi.org/10.5195/jwsr.2018.629.

Wilson, S. A. 2015. "Corporate Social Responsibility and Power Relations: Impediments to Community Development in Post-war Sierra Leone Diamond and Rutile Mining Areas." *The Extractive Industries and Society* 2(4): 704–713. https://doi.org/10.1016/j.exis.2015.09.002.

Wilson, S. A. 2013. "Company–Community Conflicts over Diamond Resources in Kono District, Sierra Leone." *Society & Natural Resources* 26(3): 254–269. https://doi.org/10.1080/08941920.2012.684849.

Wilson, N. W., and Marmo, V. 1958. "Geology, Geomorphology and Mineral Resources of the Sula Mountains." Bulletin of the Geological Survey of Sierra Leone, 1. Government Printer, Freetown, Sierra Leone.

Winnebah, T. R. A. 2006. "Social and Economic Analysis from a 360 Perspective: Report on the Sierra Rutile Ltd (SRL) Mines Area, Southern Province Sierra Leone." Department of Geography and Rural Development, School of Environmental Sciences, Njala University, Sierra Leone.

Wohlwend B. 1978. Water Legislation in Sierra Leone. Consultancy Report to FAO-UNDP SIL/73/002/LRSP-MAF.

138   CULTURE AND CONFLICTS IN SIERRA LEONE MINING

WoME. 2021. "Assessment of the Socioeconomic Impact of Artisanal Mining on Women in Sierra Leone." Women on Mining and Extractives (WoME). https://internationalwim.org/wp-content/uploads/2021/11/ASM-Sierra-Leone.pdf.

WorleyParsons. 2010. "African Minerals Limited Tonkolili Iron Ore Project: Stage 1 Environmental, Social and Health Impact Assessment." 305000-00006-0000-EN-REP-0020 18 Jun 2010.

Young, P. E. 1937. "Diamond Mines Offer a Great Challenge." *The Evangel.* May 1937.

Zack-Williams, A. 1995. *Tributors, Supporters and Merchant Capital.* Vermont: Ashgate Publishing Co.

Ziai, A. 2017. "Post-Development 25 Years after the Development Dictionary." *Third World Quarterly* 38(12): 2547–2558. https://doi.org/10.1080/01436597.2017.1383853.

https://sierraloaded.sl/news/sierra-leones-president-julius-maada-bio-coronates-eight-paramount-chiefs-encourages-peace-ambassadors/.

INDEX

Abraham, Arthur 113
actor-network theory 19
ADMS (*See* Alluvial Diamond Mining
    Scheme (ADMS))
AETC (*See* African and Eastern Trading
    Corporation (AETC))
African and Eastern Trading Corporation
    (AETC) 29
African Charter on Human and Peoples'
    Rights 31
African Minerals Ltd. (AML) 25, 71, 73,
    81, 102
African Mining Vision (AMV) 12, 15
African Railway and Port Services 33
Afro-Asia Mining Corp. Ltd. 33
AGMS (*See* Alluvial Gold Mining
    Scheme (AGMS))
agricultural lands 78, 79, 82, 93
The Aliens (Control in Special Areas)
    Ordinance 42
The Aliens (Expulsion) Ordinance 42
Alldridge, Thomas Joshua 24
Alluvial Diamond Mining
    Scheme (ADMS) 53, 54
Alluvial Gold Mining Scheme (AGMS)
    40, 53–55, 57
Alluvial Mining Ordinance 49
amalgamation method 80
American Missionary Association 24, 68
amines 85
AML (*See* African Minerals Ltd. (AML))
Amnesty International 87
AMV (*See* African Mining Vision (AMV))
ancestral rights to land 7, 102, 117
annual rent, provision for 51
Anti-Bribery and Corruption Policy 51
ARISE Integrated Industrial Platforms
    Ltd. 33

arrests 48–50, 58, 82
arsenic 81
artisanal and small scale mining (ASM)
    13, 15, 80
artisanal mining 5, 10, 14, 16, 32, 34, 38,
    41, 52, 55, 56, 58, 59, 65, 66, 101,
    115, 117
    child labor in 108
    importance of 15
    indigenous 20–25
    protest right to 117
    self-funded groups 24
artisans 7
asbestos 27
ASM (*See* artisanal and small scale
    mining (ASM))
authoritarianism 111
autochthony 8, 116
Awoko Newspaper 75

Bair, J. 11
barium 81
bauxite 20, 27, 70, 78
bilharzia 77
blacksmiths 7, 22, 24, 101
blood diamond war 19
Bondo 7, 22, 73
Boone, Sylvia Ardyn 66, 67, 73
British Titans Products (BTP) Company
    Ltd. 31
Buen vivir 12
Bumbuna Hydroelectric Project 71
burial places 68, 70

cadmium 81
capitalism 9, 12
capitalist civilizational project 6
CAST (*See* Consolidated African Selection
    Trust (CAST))

CCMS (*See* Cooperative Contract Mining Scheme (CCMS))
CDA (*See* Community Development Agreements (CDA))
CDF (*See* Colonial Development Fund (CDF))
charcoal 24
cheap labor exploitation 5
children, in mining 107–9
Children's Welfare and Community Development Programme (CWADEP) 93
China 5
Chinese miners 33, 58, 79, 82, 97
Christian missionaries 64
chromite 27
chromium 20, 26, 27
citizens/noncitizens diamond dealers' licenses 40
citizenship 8, 116
class 99, 103, 116
cobalt 36
Colonial Development and Welfare Act of 1929 28, 29
Colonial Development Fund (CDF) 29
colonial legacy 4, 5, 114–16
coltan 33, 38, 58, 78
columbite-tantalite 20, 27
commodity chains 1, 6, 11, 13
  cheap labor exploitation 5
  culture-centered 13–16
  mineral resources 4
community cohesion 7, 62, 107
Community Development Agreements (CDA) 95, 116
community-based conflict 61
Consolidated African Selection Trust (CAST) 30
Conteh, Sorie J. 71
Control of Strangers Orders 45, 48, 49
Cooperative Contract Mining Scheme (CCMS) 53
copper 20, 27
corporate social responsibility (CSR) 34, 51, 75, 102–7, 116
CSR (*See* corporate social responsibility (CSR))
cultivation 36, 71, 93
cultural alienation 13, 14, 72, 73

cultural conflicts 10, 14, 34, 35, 41, 61, 62, 71, 116
cultural continuity 7
cultural disruption 6, 13, 14, 52, 57, 72, 73, 76, 88–91
cultural evolution 7, 13, 14, 51, 79, 80, 117
cultural hybridity 6, 13, 16, 42, 51, 57, 115, 117
cultural imperialism 42, 57, 79, 101
cultural norms 10, 47, 49, 52, 56, 61, 79
Cultural Policy in Sierra Leone (Abraham) 113
cultural resistance 6, 10, 12–14, 16, 34, 115, 117
  and illicit mining 52–62
cultural sensitivity 70, 76, 91–96
cultural sustainability 6, 8, 23, 62, 72, 73, 117
cultural unequal exchange 6, 15, 16, 79, 115, 116
cultural universalism 6, 16, 115, 118
culture-centered mineral commodity chain 13–16
Customary Land Rights Act of 2022 17, 60, 108

Daily Mail (newspaper) 43
dams 31, 79, 82, 87, 88, 90
Dayu Investment Ltd. H.M. Diamonds 33
Development of the Minamata Initial Assessment (MIA) 80
Diamond Industry Policy and Management (DIPAM) Program 56
Diamond Industry Protection Ordinance 42–44, 49
Diamond Mining and Kono Religious Institutions (Conteh) 71
diamonds 14, 19, 20, 23, 27, 28, 30, 31, 33, 38, 47, 66, 70, 78
  dealer licenses 40
  illegal possession of 49
  smuggling 61
DIPAM (*See* Diamond Industry Policy and Management (DIPAM))
Downey, Liam 5
drainage systems 78
dredging operation 30, 68, 70, 78, 82
dry mining 78, 87, 104
dual governance system 4, 45, 114, 118
Dunaway, Wilma 6

INDEX

Ebola 4

ECA (*See* Economic Commission of Africa (ECA))

ecological resources 14, 34, 76, 79, 107, 116

ecological unequal exchange 5, 11, 15, 116

Economic Commission of Africa (ECA) 92

Economic Community of West African States (ECOWAS) 15, 41

economic unequal exchange 4, 5, 11, 15, 116

ECOWAS (*See* Economic Community of West African States (ECOWAS))

Ecuador 12

Edozie, R. K. 12

EIA (*See* Environmental Impact Assessment (EIA))

EITI (*See* Extractive Industries Transparency Initiative (EITI))

Environment Protection Agency Act 2022 78, 92

Environment Protection Agency-Sierra Leone (EPA-SL) 82

Environmental and Scientific Consulting Group (ESCG) 88

environmental degradation 5, 14, 78–88, 92, 93

environmental deterioration 77, 78

Environmental Impact Assessment (EIA) 87, 92

Environmental Protection Agency–Sierra Leone (EPA-SL) 78, 80, 92, 93

Environmental, Social and Health Impact Assessments (ESHIA) 59, 61, 71, 77, 78, 81, 92

envoys/rulers 7

EPA-SL (*See* Environment Protection Agency-Sierra Leone (EPA-SL))

ESCG (*See* Environmental and Scientific Consulting Group (ESCG))

ESHIA (*See* Environmental, Social and Health Impact Assessments (ESHIA))

ethnic identity 13

Etxano, I. 12

Eurocentric/Western-centric knowledge 9, 13

Evangelical United Brethren Church 68

ex-combatants 8, 22

extraction method 78, 80

Extractive Industries Transparency Initiative (EITI) 15, 51, 59

farming 5, 10, 22–24, 34, 36, 52, 81, 88, 93–95, 97, 101, 109

FDI (*See* foreign direct investment (FDI))

fele nets 88, 90

Ferme, Marianne 90

FESS (*See* Foundation for Environmental Security and Sustainability (FESS))

fishing 34, 81, 88–90, 93, 109 (*See also* scoop-net fishing)

foreign direct investment (FDI) 4, 12, 17
in land 7

Foundation for Environmental Security and Sustainability (FESS) 72

Fowler-Lunn, Katherine 27, 70, 80, 97, 100, 101

Framework and Guidelines on Land Policy 9

Frank, B. 8

Friends of the Earth 69, 106

Fulas 52

Fyfe, Christopher 113

Gado 24

garnet 27

gasoline 78, 80

Gbangbama Hill 68

Gbangbani 7, 22, 71

GCGS (*See* Gold Coast Geological Survey (GCGS))

gender relationships 6, 8, 90, 99, 107, 116

GGDO (*See* Government Gold and Diamond Office (GGDO))

Ghanaian 37

God: Ancestor or Creator? (Sawyerr) 63

The Gold Missus: A Woman Prospector in Sierra Leone (Fowler-Lunn) 80

Gola Rainforest National Park (GRNP) 75

gold (mining) 6, 14–16, 20, 23–25, 27, 30, 33, 38, 78–80, 95, 100
extraction operations 79
land degradation 91
land reclamation 91
license holders in 39
rights 25, 51, 54, 55, 58

Gold Coast Geological Survey (GCGS) 27

Gottschalk, K. 12

Government Gold and Diamond Office (GGDO) 41

graphite 27
Greco, Elisa 12
greeting kola 27
GRNP (*See* Gola Rainforest National Park (GRNP))
Guinea 1, 21, 25, 43, 47

Harbottle, Michael 50
Hargreaves, John 35
Harris, W. T. 65
healers 7
herbalists 7
hiring practices 102–7
A History of Sierra Leone (Fyfe) 156
Humoi 66
hunters 7
hydrochloric acid 85
hydrogen fluoride 85

IDMP (*See* Integrated Diamond Mining Programme (IDMP))
IFC Performance Standards on Environmental and Social Sustainability 15
illegal diamond miners 19, 50, 59
illicit/illegal mining 14, 42–45, 48, 49, 52–62, 58, 61, 71, 72, 74, 76, 78, 91, 92, 117
ilmenite 20, 27, 82, 87
The Immigration Restriction Ordinance of 1946 42, 43
Imperi Hill 68
Imperial College of Science and Technology 28
imprisonment 49, 54, 105
incorporation process 6
indigenous artisanal mining 20–25
Influx Management Plan 61
in-migrant farmers 7
Integrated Diamond Mining Programme (IDMP) 56
Invest Salone 60
iron 20
iron ore 20, 22, 24, 25, 27–29, 70, 72, 78

Jong River 82
Julas 16, 23

Kangari Hills 30, 80, 81
Kimberley Process Certification Scheme 15

Kingho Investment Co. 33
kinship rights to land 7, 8
The Knave of Diamonds (Harbottle) 50
Komahun Gold Processing Plant 81
Kono District Council 47
Kono District Order 47, 49
Kono Tribal Authorities 47
Kpanguima 66
Kurumasaba 63

Lake Confon (*See* Lake Sonfon)
Lake Sonfon 23, 65, 74, 80–82, 95, 100
land degradation 91
land governance systems 1, 7, 13, 50, 59, 60
land management 1, 7, 11, 16, 17, 33–36, 61, 62, 65, 103, 115, 116
land reclamation 72, 91, 92, 104
land rehabilitation 91, 92, 104
land rights 1, 5, 10, 11, 35, 52, 60, 76, 93, 102–7 (*See also* ancestral rights to land)
land use 1, 5, 7, 10, 14, 29, 34, 36, 51, 72, 79, 100, 108, 114, 116, 118
landlord-indigenes 11, 14, 23, 24, 51, 52, 65, 73, 79, 94, 95, 99, 102, 106, 112
  ancestral lands of 41
  compensation 87
  cultural beliefs 104
  customary rights 35
  mining lease 38
  rights to govern land 37
  share in rice harvest 23
landlord-stranger institution 1, 9–11, 13, 22, 23, 36, 59, 60, 103, 115
landlord-stranger relationship 8, 13, 17, 36, 52, 76, 116
large scale mining 4, 15, 19, 32, 33, 38, 79
  agreements for 32
lasmami 88
laws and regulations 91–96
lead 20, 81
leases to mining 15, 34, 36, 41, 69, 91, 114
Lebanese 38, 40, 43–45, 50–52
legal mining 14
Leone Rock Metal Group (*See* Kingho Investment Co.)
Liberia 43
license holders 38, 39, 41, 50, 54, 103, 107
license, mining (*See* mining license)
lignite 27

INDEX

livelihoods 7, 8, 14, 22, 34, 62, 65, 79, 82,
 88, 90, 95, 98, 117
 agricultural communities depended 22
 artisanal mining and farming 101
 of indigenous people 5
 loss of 78
 for young people 56
London Mining Agreement 2012 70
London Mining Company (LMC) 75
loss of land 5, 103

Mabesi lake 65
Malaysians 104
Mali 11, 15, 43
Mamdani, M. 10
Mami Wata 108
Mande-Jula system of extraction 23
Mannathukkaren, N. 9
Mape lake 65
marabouts 7
Maraka 23, 38, 47, 52
Marmo, Vladi 25
Maroc Co. Ltd. 27, 30, 41, 55
Mawuru River 81
mbembei nets 88, 90
Mbogboni 66
Mende ethnic group 105
mercury 80
Meya Mining 33
MIA (*See* Development of the
 Minamata Initial Assessment (MIA))
mineral exploration 25, 27–29, 31, 32, 81
mineral resources 28, 29, 31, 75
 in African development 12
 exploitation of 92
 extraction of 4
 villages to access 88
mineral rights 29, 32, 35
Minerals Amendment Ordinance of
 1947 91
Minerals Ordinance of 1927 25, 29, 31,
 41, 70, 109
Minerals Ordinance of 1931 42
Mines and Mineral Act of 2009 93
Mines and Mineral Development Act
 2021 15, 108
mining
 children in 107–9
 in colonial and postcolonial eras 25–34

conflicts 1
development 16–17, 51, 104
environmental deterioration from
 79–88
illicit 14, 42–45, 48, 49, 52–62, 91, 117
land use 51
legal 14
regulations 91–96
sociopolitical structures 37
trade 51
waste 80, 87
women in 107–9
mining lease (*See* leases to mining)
mining license 24, 32, 38, 40, 41, 50, 52,
 53, 91
 citizens and noncitizens 40
mining policy 15, 50, 74, 118
mining rights, gold 25, 51, 54, 55, 58
Mitchell, Harry 48, 49
MNC (*See* Multinational Corporations
 (MNC))
Moa River 30, 66
Moinde River 72
Moindema Lake 72
molybdenum 20
monazite 20, 27
monetary loans 24, 102
Moore H.L. 8
Multinational Corporations (MNC) 5,
 10–14
musicians 7

NAMATI 60
National Action Plan (NAP) 80
National Land Commission Act of 2022
 16, 60
National Land Policy (NLP) 22, 59, 114
National Reparation Programme 66
Natural Resource Charter 15
natural resource extraction 5
neoextractivism 12
Ngewo 63
nickel 20, 26
Niger 15
Nigeria 11, 96
nitric acid 80
NLP (*See* National Land Policy (NLP))
Northern Mercantile and Investment
 Corporation (NMIC) 29

onchocerciasis 77
oppression 9, 108, 111, 116
Organization for Research and Extension
    of Intermediate Technology
    (OREINT) 69, 106

Pampana Mining Co. 81
Pampana River 30, 65, 80, 81, 95
pastoralists 7
Peace Diamond Alliance (PDA) 56
Perinbam, B. M. 15
Peters, Pauline 8
platinum 27
political economy 19
pollution control 68, 91, 92
poro 35, 36
poverty 58, 106, 108, 117
Powell Duffryn Steam Coal Company
    Ltd. 27
The Practice of Presence (Sawyerr) 63
Protectorate Land Ordinance of 1905 4
Protectorate Land Ordinance of 1927 36,
    51, 60
Protectorate Ordinance of 1897 35
Provinces Land Ordinance of 1933 36
pyrochlore 20

race 8, 99, 100, 116
*Radiance from the Waters: Ideals of Feminine
    Beauty in Mende Art* (Boone) 66
railway 29, 31, 33, 108
refugees 8, 22
Revolutionary United Front of
    Sierra Leone (RUF/SL) 8, 19, 22,
    50, 59, 66, 90, 94, 102
rice cultivation 88, 105
Richards, Paul 105
river blindness 77
Rodney, Walter 5
Rokel River 30, 80, 95
Rosen, D.M. 107
RUF/SL (*See* Revolutionary United Front
    of Sierra Leone (RUF/SL))
RUF/SL Blood Diamond War
    (1991–2001) 12
rutile 20, 27, 82, 87
    extraction 70

sacred bush 24, 63, 67, 70–73, 75
sacred places 7, 8, 14, 62, 63, 65, 66,
    70–72, 74, 76, 116, 117

safe disposal of waste 92
salary scale 5, 92
Sande 7, 22, 66, 73, 90, 91, 107
Sanders, T 8
Sawyerr, Harry 63
    God: Ancestor or Creator? 63
    The Practice of Presence 63
schistosomiasis 77
scoop-net fishing 66, 88–91
selenium 81
self-funded groups 24
Senegal 43
SEPL (*See* Special Exclusive Prospecting
    License (SEPL))
Sewa River 30, 66
Shack, W.A. 10
shakehand 22
Sierra Diamonds Ltd. 33
Sierra Leone Development Company
    (SLDC) 29–31, 33, 94, 95, 97, 99,
    101, 102
Sierra Leone Extractive Industries
    Transparency Initiative (SLEITI) 59
Sierra Leone Geological Survey (SLGS)
    25, 26, 28, 31, 78
Sierra Leone Minerals Policy 2018 15, 61
Sierra Leone Progressive Independence
    Movement (SLPIM) 47, 48
Sierra Leone Selection Trust (SLST) 30,
    41–44, 48–50, 53, 57, 58, 65, 71, 72,
    98, 99, 101, 106
Sierra Rutile Agreement of 2002 31, 38,
    51, 82, 93
Sierra Rutile Ltd. (SRL) 37, 51, 61, 73–75,
    102–4, 106
Skinner, E.P. 10
slave trading 111
SLDC (*See* Sierra Leone Development
    Company (SLDC))
SLEITI (*See* Sierra Leone Extractive
    Industries Transparency Initiative
    (SLEITI))
SLGS (*See* Sierra Leone Geological
    Survey (SLGS))
SLPIM (*See* Sierra Leone Progressive
    Independence Movement (SLPIM))
SLST (*See* Sierra Leone Selection Trust
    (SLST))
small-scale mining 78

INDEX

smugglers 38, 44
smuggling 44, 61, 74, 117
soapstone 26
social protests 61
sodium hydroxide 85
soil conservation 54, 79, 91
Solondo 68
Sonfon lake 65
Special Exclusive Prospecting License
(SEPL) 29–31
spirituality 62
vs. land 9
vs. nature 63
SRL (*See* Sierra Rutile Ltd. (SRL))
stranger/s 7, 10, 11, 16, 24, 37, 38, 43, 47,
78, 99 (*See also* landlord-stranger
institution)
artisans 7
envoys or rulers 7
ex combatants 8
healers 7
herbalists 7
hunters 7
in-migrant farmers 7
marabouts 7
musicians 7
pastoralists 7
refugees 8
traders 7
uprooted migrants 7
Sula Mountains 23, 25, 30, 65, 80, 81, 95
sulphuric acid 85
Syrians 38, 43, 45

terrorism 111
Thompson, George E. 24, 68, 90
tin 20
titanium 26, 31, 82
Tonkolili Agreement of 1933 94
topaz 27
traders 7, 16, 22–24, 35, 37, 38, 56, 107
Tribal Authorities Ordinance of
1938 90
Tribal Authorities Ordinance of 1958
44, 47
Truth and Reconciliation Commission
(TRC) 66

UAC (*See* United Africa Company (UAC))
Ubuntu 12

UNECA (*See* United Nations
Economic Commission for
Africa (UNECA))
UN Guiding Principles for Business and
Human Rights (UNGP) 15, 88
unequal ecological exchange (*See*
ecological unequal exchange)
United Africa Company (UAC) 29
United Methodist Church (*See* Evangelical
United Brethren Church)
United Nations Economic Commission
for Africa (UNECA) 31
United States 5, 96
universalization, culture and knowledge
production 6
unoccupied lands 36
uprooted migrants 7

vanadium 20
Villalba-Eguiluz, C.U. 12
vivir bien 12

wage labor 14, 37, 98, 99, 103
Wallerstein, Immanuel 6
water quality 87, 88
water rights 29–31
water sources 34, 93, 116
Western Europe 4, 5
WHO (*See* World Health Organization
(WHO))
Wilson, N.W. 25
women
fishing 88–91
in mining 107–9
Women on Mining and Extractives–
Sierra Leone (WoME-SL) 95, 108
World Bank 4, 17
World Health Organization (WHO)
81, 88
Wunde 7, 22

Xin Tai Mining Co. Ltd. 33

Yataa 63
Yemen Co. Ltd. 80
Young, Parker E. 64

Ziai, A. 12
zinc 20
zircon 20, 27, 38, 58, 78, 82, 85
Zircon Wet Plant 85

Printed in the USA
CPSIA information can be obtained
at www.ICGtesting.com
JSHW022054100224
56871JS00013B/6